Table of Content[s]

Steps for Learning Spelling Words

1. Look carefully at the spelling word.

2. Say the spelling word out loud.
   • How many syllables do you hear?
   • What consonant sounds do you hear?
   • What vowel sounds do you hear?

3. Check the word for spelling patterns.

4. Spell the word out loud.

5. Cover the spelling word.

6. Write the spelling word from memory.

7. Check the spelling word.

8. Repeat as needed.

Say each word out loud. Listen for the short *a* sound.

Copy and spell each word three times using colours of your choice.

1. canyon _____ _____ _____

2. fasten _____ _____ _____

3. accept _____ _____ _____

4. hangar _____ _____ _____

5. detach _____ _____ _____

6. janitor _____ _____ _____

7. packet _____ _____ _____

8. banjo _____ _____ _____

9. example _____ _____ _____

10. knack _____ _____ _____

Brain Stretch

- Create a word search puzzle based on the spelling words.
- On a piece of paper, write a sentence using each spelling word.

| accept | banjo | canyon | detach | example |
| fasten | hangar | janitor | knack | packet |

1. Fill in the blank using the best spelling word from the list.

a) The actors will go onstage to _____ awards and make speeches.

b) Mom makes sure I _____ my seatbelt before she drives away.

c) Bo has a _____ for knowing the right thing to say in most situations.

d) The plane taxied slowly into the _____ to get repaired.

e) My Aunt Carrie is really good at playing the _____.

f) Our youth group is going hiking in the _____ this weekend.

g) To use the key card, you must _____ it from the main card first.

h) My Uncle Fred was a _____ at the elementary school.

i) Grandma ripped open a _____ of sugar to put in her tea.

j) Trilliums are an _____ of a well-known Ontario wildflower.

Brain Stretch

How many spelling words can you fit into one sentence and still make sense?
Give it a try!

1. The word below is spelled incorrectly. Write the correct spelling on the line.

    a) paquet _____

    b) fassen _____

    c) hangur _____

    d) detatch _____

    e) bandjo _____

    f) janetor _____

    g) canion _____

    h) eksampull _____

2. Unscramble the spelling word. Write the word on the line.

    a) cnkak _____

    b) tasfne _____

    c) thadce _____

    d) granah _____

    e) pmaxele _____

    f) ijnaort _____

    g) ycnano _____

    h) cepatc _____

3. Circle the word with the short *a* sound that makes the most sense.

   Write the word in the sentence.

    a) Cindy hurt her _____ in gym class today. (apple   ankle)

    b) Devon is very _____ about how his painting turned out. (happy   angry)

    c) Robby _____ a mosquito on his arm. (scratched   smacked)

    d) Jessy _____ reads before she goes to bed. (always   accidentally)

    e) Max is _____ spaghetti for dinner tonight. (hating   having)

accept	banjo	canyon	detach	example
fasten	hangar	janitor	knack	packet

1. Write the correct spelling word from the list to match the clue.

   a) A person who cleans buildings for a living   _____

   b) A stringed musical instrument with a long neck and
      a round body with an open back   _____

   c) An acquired or natural skill at doing, or a tendency
      to do, something specific   _____

   d) A large building for housing aircraft   _____

   e) To unfasten something and separate it from an object _____

   f) Something characteristic of its kind or showing a rule _____

   g) A small package   _____

   h) To close or join something securely   _____

   i) A deep gorge, usually with a river flowing through it _____

   j) To believe something, or to agree to receive something _____

2. Underline the words that have a short **a** sound.

   a) tasty   track   crane   past   half   smear

   b) cackle   blank   drape   shear   fairy   habitat

   c) careful   laugh   shame   crayon   splash   crabby

Say each word out loud. Listen for the short **e** sound.

Copy and spell each word three times using colours of your choice.

1. venom _____ _____ _____

2. regular _____ _____ _____

3. exercise _____ _____ _____

4. television _____ _____ _____

5. sketch _____ _____ _____

6. impatient _____ _____ _____

7. medicine _____ _____ _____

8. shorten _____ _____ _____

9. petition _____ _____ _____

10. quartet _____ _____ _____

Spelling Tip

The short **e** sound can be spelled with **ai** (*said*) or **ie** (*friend*)

exercise	impatient	medicine	petition	quartet
regular	shorten	sketch	television	venom

1. Fill in the blank using the best spelling word from the list.

a) It's a good idea to _____ for at least 30 minutes each day.

b) The doctor gave my father _____ to help me get well again.

c) When I see a squirrel, I always _____ Teddy's leash to control him.

d) I love to draw buildings, animals, and scenery in my _____ book.

e) My little brother is very _____ when waiting to open presents.

f) A Mississauga rattlesnake has very poisonous _____.

g) We started a _____ to ask for a park in our neighbourhood.

h) My grandfather was a singer in a barber shop _____.

i) The shapes are arranged in a _____ pattern of squares and circles.

j) My favourite shows are on _____ weekday afternoons.

Brain Stretch

How many spelling words can you fit into one sentence and still make sense? Give it a try!

Spelling Week 2 – Word Study

1. Underline the words that have a short *e* sound.

   a) special   sweet   propel   sliver   letter   peat

   b) eyelash   spending   fresher   monkey   feather   melt

   c) grove   fender   squeal   lemon   recycle   health

   d) barrette   shred   green   peach   elephant   maker

   e) friend   merry   sheep   crept   weight   vest

2. Circle the word with the short *e* sound that makes the most sense.

   Write the word in the sentence.

   a) In her dream, Kelly _____ like she was flying over the rooftops. (felt   knelt)

   b) The technician made a _____ of the pipes to show my dad. (fetch   sketch)

   c) Mom put the box of cereal up in the kitchen _____. (cabinet   carpet)

   d) The cat _____ silently into the bushes to hunt for bugs. (slept   crept)

3. The word *fell* can have two meanings.

   Write a sentence to show each meaning of the word *fell*.

   _____

   _____

Spelling Week 2 – Word Study

exercise	impatient	medicine	petition	quartet
regular	shorten	sketch	television	venom

1. Write the correct spelling word from the list to match the clue.

a) A document signed by a lot of people to ask an

   official body for or to do a specific thing   _____

b) A poisonous substance produced by a snake   _____

c) A device that transmits sound and images   _____

d) A rough or unfinished drawing   _____

e) To make or become shorter   _____

f) A definite pattern; or occuring at equal intervals   _____

g) Activity requiring physical effort, and carried out to

   maintain or improve health and fitness   _____

h) A group of four people playing music or singing together _____

i) A preparation used for the treatment or prevention of

   disease or to cure illness   _____

j) Restlessly eager   _____

2. Write a word that rhymes with the given word. The rhyming words do not have to be

   spelled in the same way.

a) spell _____   b) health _____   c) slept _____

Say each word out loud. Listen for the short *i* sound.

Copy and spell each word three times using colours of your choice.

1. skillet _____ _____ _____

2. ignore _____ _____ _____

3. cabinet _____ _____ _____

4. fossil _____ _____ _____

5. accident _____ _____ _____

6. listening _____ _____ _____

7. predict _____ _____ _____

8. official _____ _____ _____

9. resident _____ _____ _____

10. exhibit _____ _____ _____

Brain Stretch

- Create a word search puzzle based on the spelling words.
- On a piece of paper, write a sentence using each spelling word.

Spelling Week 3 – Words with a Short *i* Sound

| accident | cabinet | exhibit | fossil | ignore |
| listening | official | predict | resident | skillet |

1. Fill in the blank using the best spelling word from the list.

a) My uncle likes to _____ which baseball team will win the game.

b) Nia's brother had an _____ and damaged the car quite badly.

c) The box of crackers is in the kitchen _____ on the far right.

d) I found a trilobyte _____ in the parking lot at the beach today.

e) The _____ word on the fireworks display is that it will be at 10:00 p.m.

f) Grandma is a _____ of the seniors' apartment in our town.

g) Dad is making delicious homefries in the _____.

h) My mother is _____ to country music while she's cooking dinner.

i) I'm excited to see the mummy _____ at the museum tomorrow.

j) If Greg keeps bothering you, just try to _____ him.

Brain Stretch

How many spelling words can you fit into one sentence and still make sense?
Give it a try!

Spelling Week 3 – Word Study

1. Circle the word with the short *i* sound that makes the most sense.

   Write the word in the sentence.

   a) It's hard to _____ how huge the universe is. (include   imagine)

   b) Mike is reading the new Batman _____. (picnic   comic)

   c) We look for salamanders under the wooden _____. (bridge   fidget)

2. Homophones are words that sound the same but are spelled differently.

   Write the homophone for the given word.

   a) practise _____

   b) missed _____

   c) witch _____

   d) gilt _____

   e) links _____

   f) wring _____

3. How many syllables does the word have? Write the number beside the word.

   a) friendship _____

   b) hippopotamus _____

   c) distance _____

4. Write a word that rhymes with the word below. The word does not have to be spelled the same to rhyme.

   a) spilled _____

   b) skit _____

   c) gift _____

   d) mitten _____

   e) skitter _____

   f) grip _____

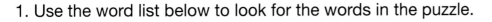

1. Use the word list below to look for the words in the puzzle.

   Circle the word in the word search puzzle. Then cross out the word in the list.

C	B	I	S	C	U	I	T	K
R	F	R	D	R	P	M	T	I
I	R	I	S	E	N	W	R	T
M	M	P	Z	R	U	I	I	T
I	U	T	O	Z	P	N	M	E
N	F	L	X	I	Y	D	S	N
A	F	I	F	D	I	Y	N	E
L	I	M	M	I	S	K	I	N
B	N	i	U	D	R	I	F	T
L	D	T	I	P	X	U	F	Z

biscuit	**criminal**	**drift**	**fizzy**	**kitten**	**limit**
muffin	**risen**	**skin**	**sniff**	**trims**	**windy**

2. Unscramble the spelling word. Write the correct spelling on the line.

a) tklisle _____

b) gronie _____

c) dcpriet _____

d) ficolaif _____

e) hbtixei _____

f) ncbaiet_____

Spelling Week 4 – Words with a Short *o* Sound

Say each word out loud. Listen for the short **o** sound.

Copy and spell each word three times using colours of your choice.

1. solve _____ _____ _____

2. adopt _____ _____ _____

3. following _____ _____ _____

4. copier _____ _____ _____

5. involve _____ _____ _____

6. coffee _____ _____ _____

7. voluntary _____ _____ _____

8. bonnet _____ _____ _____

9. project _____ _____ _____

10. blonde _____ _____ _____

Brain Stretch

- Create a word search puzzle based on the spelling words.
- On a piece of paper, write a sentence using each spelling word.

| adopt | blonde | bonnet | coffee | copier |
| following | involve | project | solve | voluntary |

1. Fill in the blank using the best spelling word from the list.

a) My family is going to _____ a dog at the animal shelter today.

b) Kim's science _____ is about the formation of the solar system.

c) The big _____ broke down, so I can't get a copy of this map.

d) Aunt Amy's baby has extremely _____ hair.

e) The detective works hard to _____ his cases.

f) Participation in the annual river cleanup is completely _____.

g) The baby is wearing a pink _____ with bunnies on it.

h) Jack is brewing a pot of _____ for his guests.

i) This trip to the beach will _____ swimming and a picnic lunch.

j) Lily is _____ a famous singer on Instagram.

Brain Stretch

How many spelling words can you fit into one sentence and still make sense?
Give it a try!

Spelling Week 4 – Word Study

1. Circle the word with the short **o** sound that makes the most sense.

   Write the word in the sentence.

   a) Trish is trying to _____ a mystery. (connect   solve)

   b) My family wants to _____ a little girl or boy. (adopt   follow)

   c) I'm making a volcano for my science _____. (model   project)

   d) We gave the baby a cute _____ with a kitten on it. (bonnet   locket)

2. Write a word that rhymes with the given word. The rhyming word does not have to be spelled in the same way.

   a) propped _____   b) sock _____   c) stop _____

   d) trot _____   e) moss _____   f) gone _____

   g) solve _____   h) follow _____   i) copy _____

3. Circle the words that have a short **o** sound.

   a) drool   bossy   shower   tonic   goat   softly

   b) tropical   rough   cross   post   town   fought

   c) shoes   rocket   brought   ghost   sparrow   fossil

adopt	blonde	bonnet	coffee	copier
following	involve	project	solve	voluntary

1. Write the correct spelling word from the list to match the clue.

a) Having light or pale yellow hair _____

b) To include something or someone as a necessary
   part of an event or result _____

c) A carefully planned and designed undertaking _____

d) To legally take another person's child and raise it
   as one's own _____

e) A brimmed hat that ties under the chin _____

f) Machine that makes exact copies of a document _____

g) Done through one's own choice or agreement _____

h) Maintaining awareness of the current state or progress
   of something or someone _____

i) A hot drink made from roasted and ground coffee beans _____

j) Find an answer to or explanation for something _____

2. Unscramble the spelling word. Write the correct spelling on the line.

a) cpjoret _____

b) pdoat _____

c) dloebn _____

d) vilenov _____

e) fcoefe _____

f) pciore _____

Say each word out loud. Look at the different letters that make the short *u* sound.

Copy and spell each word three times using colours of your choice.

1. luggage _____ _____ _____

2. punish _____ _____ _____

3. button _____ _____ _____

4. sculptor _____ _____ _____

5. crutch _____ _____ _____

6. muscle _____ _____ _____

7. culture _____ _____ _____

8. plumber _____ _____ _____

9. support _____ _____ _____

10. tuxedo _____ _____ _____

Spelling Tip

Words with *o* can have a short *u* sound (*Monday, month, mother*).

Spelling Week 5 – Words with a Short *u* Sound

button	crutch	culture	luggage	muscle
plumber	punish	sculptor	support	tuxedo

1. Fill in the blank using the best spelling word from the list.

a) Mom said we shouldn't _____ the puppy when he pees on the floor.

b) Each week at school, we try new foods from a different _____.

c) The town gathered a lot of _____ for the hurricane victims.

d) Mom filled the _____ with clothes and snacks for the long trip.

e) The _____ carved a beautiful statue out of marble.

f) Perry likes to press the floor _____ in the elevator.

g) The _____ has come to fix the kitchen sink.

h) A _____ helps you move parts of your body, such as your leg.

i) My uncle wore a nice black _____ on his wedding day.

j) Lexi broke her leg and had to use a _____ to walk.

Brain Stretch

How many spelling words can you fit into one sentence and still make sense?
Give it a try!

1. Circle the words that do **not** have a short *u* sound.

a) munch   proud   touch   rough   through

b) scuttle   mutton   pounce   trusty   cough

c) muck   about   fruit   sponge   plunge

d) touch   thump   rumple   though   guest

2. Add a letter or letters to form a word with a short *u* sound. Write the word on the line.

a) _____under   _____   b) _____ove   _____

c) _____uff   _____   d) _____uddle   _____

e) _____umble   _____   f) _____ough   _____

3. Unscramble the spelling word. Write the correct spelling on the line.

a) etudxo   _____   b) psucltro   _____

c) tercluu   _____   d) slmuce   _____

e) hcurtc   _____   f) ubtotn   _____

g) mpeublr _____   h) glgageu   _____

i) spniuh   _____

1. Use the word list below to look for the words in the puzzle.

   Circle the word in the word search puzzle. Then cross out the word in the list.

P	U	D	D	L	E	T	T	S
O	L	T	D	F	M	H	U	N
B	U	U	N	L	G	U	M	U
U	N	G	C	U	U	N	B	G
T	G	R	O	F	S	D	L	G
T	S	T	U	F	T	E	E	L
O	F	H	U	G	E	R	H	E
N	F	L	U	M	B	E	R	H
C	U	S	T	A	R	D	B	J
D	R	T	T	L	T	U	G	Z

button	custard	fluff	hug	lumber	lungs
puddle	snuggle	thunder	tuft	tug	tumble

2. Write a word that rhymes with the word below. The word does not have to be spelled the same to rhyme.

   a) one _____   b) tough _____   c) yummy _____

   d) rumble _____   e) blunder _____   f) grumpy _____

Spelling Week 6 – Words with a Long *a* Sound

Say each word out loud. Listen for the long *a* sound.

Copy and spell each word three times using colours of your choice.

1. capable   _____   _____   _____

2. detail   _____   _____   _____

3. halo   _____   _____   _____

4. imitate   _____   _____   _____

5. waste   _____   _____   _____

6. grateful   _____   _____   _____

7. elevator   _____   _____   _____

8. ancient   _____   _____   _____

9. mistake   _____   _____   _____

10. gaze   _____   _____   _____

Spelling Tips: The long *a* sound can be spelled with

- letters *ai* (*quail*)
- letter *a* followed by a **consonant** + **e** (*earthquake*)
- letters *ay* (*relay*)

Spelling Week 6 – Words with a Long *a* Sound

ancient	capable	detail	elevator	gaze
grateful	halo	imitate	mistake	waste

1. Fill in the blank using the best spelling word from the list.

a) I'm _____ of doing anything I decide to try.

b) On the test, I forgot to give one important _____ about insects.

c) Our cat often sits in the window to _____ out at the birds.

d) The angel on our Christmas tree has a _____ on its head.

e) Bluejays often _____ the sounds of other birds.

f) I love to ride the _____ in Grandma's apartment building.

g) At Thanksgiving dinner, we all say what we are _____ for.

h) Food _____ is turned into compost in our yard.

i) It was a big _____ to throw out my old notebooks.

j) Gladiators fought in the Colosseum in _____ Rome.

Brain Stretch

How many spelling words can you fit into one sentence and still make sense?
Give it a try!

1. Say the word out loud. Underline the words with the long *a* sound.

   a) crate   seal   make   stale   reach

   b) stake   wall   hazy   soap   slate

   c) taste   bean   rain   unreal   frame

   d) parade   dark   lake   cheat   away

2. Look around the room. See the objects and say their names out loud. Write down as many objects as you can find that have a long *a* sound.

   _____

   _____

   _____

   _____

3. Write a short story using as many of the words as you can from Question 2.

   _____

   _____

   _____

   _____

1. Use the word list below to look for the words in the puzzle.

   Circle the word in the word search puzzle. Then cross out the word in the list.

S	T	E	A	K	B	C	L	W
G	R	A	T	E	L	E	A	A
Y	A	L	A	Z	Y	O	P	V
B	C	X	C	A	I	I	A	Y
E	H	W	I	T	S	S	R	L
A	E	T	R	A	I	N	A	G
R	Q	Y	M	M	G	D	D	E
C	R	A	T	E	R	L	E	H
I	E	M	A	I	L	M	B	J
D	R	X	R	A	Y	U	G	Z

ache   bear   crater email   grate lazy

parade steak   tame   train   wavy xray

2. Write a word that rhymes with the word below. The word does not have to be spelled the same to rhyme.

   a) fair _____   b) quake _____   c) blame _____

   d) paste _____   e) play _____   f) train _____

Say each word out loud. Look at the different letters that make the long *e* sound.

Copy and spell each word three times using colours of your choice.

1. zero _____ _____ _____

2. yield _____ _____ _____

3. beliefs _____ _____ _____

4. weevil _____ _____ _____

5. creative _____ _____ _____

6. museum _____ _____ _____

7. ceiling _____ _____ _____

8. fierce _____ _____ _____

9. release _____ _____ _____

10. defeat _____ _____ _____

Spelling Tips: The long *e* sound can be spelled with

- letter *e* by itself, and *e* followed by a **consonant** + *e* (*detach, complete*)
- letters *ee*, *ea*, and *ie* (*peel, each, shield*)
- letters *y* and *ey* (*mummy, valley*)

beliefs	creative	ceiling	defeat	fierce
museum	release	weevil	yield	zero

1. Fill in the blank using the best spelling word from the list.

a) On their wedding day, the couple will _____ doves into the air.

b) A metallic green _____ is sitting on that pink flower beside you.

c) Ice forms quickly on roads around _____ degrees Celsius.

d) This recipe will _____ 12 chocolate chip muffins.

e) Our soccer team hopes to _____ the red team tomorrow.

f) We will hang pumpkin streamers from the _____ on Halloween.

g) Lions are _____ predators that live in the African savanna.

h) The _____ in the city has an amazing dinosaur exhibit!

i) Lane draws, paints, and works with clay. She is very _____.

j) Always respect other people's _____, even if we don't share them.

Brain Stretch

How many spelling words can you fit into one sentence and still make sense?
Give it a try!

1. Unscramble the spelling word. Write the correct spelling on the line.

a) sumume _____   b) elievw _____   c) fadete _____

d) refeci _____   e) flebise _____   f) dyeli _____

g) necilgi _____   h) trivaece _____   i) sleraee_____

2. Circle the words that have a long *e* sound.

a) field   mean   pest   never   alley

b) shelter   relief   event   greet   guest

c) tweezers   bunny   cleaver   trend   festival

d) prey   steak   create   rely   quest

e) speech   clever   seek   fairy   skeleton

3. Compound words are two smaller words put together to make one bigger word.
   Draw a line between the two smaller words in the bigger word.

a) cartwheel   monkey   beachball   bicycle   earthquake

b) butter   daydream   about   seastar   fireworks

c) meadow   earlobe   fender   honeydew   stingray

d) teaspoon   thunder   timeline   ponytail   berries

| beliefs | creative | ceiling | defeat | fierce |
| museum | release | weevil | yield | zero |

1. Write the correct spelling word from the list to match the clue.

   a) The upper interior surface of a room _____

   b) Acceptance that a statement is true or something exists _____

   c) Involving imagination or original ideas, especially in art _____

   d) A small beetle with a long snout _____

   e) To produce or provide something _____

   f) No quantity or number of something; the number 0 _____

   g) Win a victory over someone in a battle or contest _____

   h) To set something free _____

   i) Physically violent or frightening _____

   j) A building in which objects of historical, scientific,
   artistic, or cultural interest are stored and exhibited _____

2. Do **not** use the spelling word list for this activity. Write 2 words that have a long *e* sound made by the following letters:

   a) ee _____   b) ie _____

   c) y _____   d) ea _____

Say each word out loud. Listen for the long *i* sound.

Copy and spell each word three times using colours of your choice.

1. crisis _____ _____ _____

2. frighten _____ _____ _____

3. knives _____ _____ _____

4. entire _____ _____ _____

5. remind _____ _____ _____

6. choir _____ _____ _____

7. fireproof _____ _____ _____

8. outline _____ _____ _____

9. invire _____ _____ _____

10. pastime _____ _____ _____

Spelling Tips: The long *i* sound can be spelled with

- letters *igh* and *ign* (*lightning, signed*)
- letter *i* followed by **consonant + e** (*while*)
- letters *ie* and *y* (*pie, spy*)

choir	crisis	entire	fireproof	frighten
invite	knives	outline	pastime	remind

1. Fill in the blank using the best spelling word from the list.

   a) My brother's purpose on Halloween is to _____ all the children.

   b) We have to create an _____ of the story we want to write.

   c) My sister is a soprano singer in the church _____.

   d) Uncle Tim uses sand as a _____ base for his firepit.

   e) A good chef always uses sharp _____ to cut food.

   f) Knitting clothing and blankets for my dolls is my favourite _____.

   g) The fundraising event helped victims of the flooding _____.

   h) When we left the kitchen for a while, our dog ate the _____ pizza.

   i) I want to _____ my classmates to my backyard pool party.

   j) Every morning, Mom has to _____ me to make my bed.

Brain Stretch

How many spelling words can you fit into one sentence and still make sense? Give it a try!

Spelling Week 8 – Word Study

1. Say the word out loud. Underline the words with the long *i* sound.

a) spine	fringe	sigh	skinny	lightning
b) slipping	bright	scary	style	fry
c) yield	signed	sprint	rhyme	write
d) chime	cycle	quick	twine	carry
e) twice	citizen	flair	fried	height

2. A **synonym** is a word that means the same as another word.

   Circle the synonym for the bolded word.

   a) **twine**   twisted   string   b) **shy**   timid   bold

3. Circle the word with the long *i* sound that makes the most sense.

   Write the word in the sentence.

   a) Mom got some new _____ for her indoor garden. (cacti   felines)

   b) I can trace the _____ of a tree with my finger. (spine   outline)

   c) Dad will polish the car until it _____. (shines   whines)

   d) The teacher _____ us all to a barbecue Saturday. (frightened   invited)

   e) I like to _____ the tree in our backyard. (climb   wipe)

1. Use the word list below to look for the words in the puzzle.

   Circle the word in the word search puzzle. Then cross out the word in the list.

S	P	R	I	T	E	T	K	W
G	R	I	N	D	C	I	N	H
Y	C	K	A	Z	Y	L	I	I
C	G	I	C	A	C	E	F	N
Y	H	I	O	T	L	S	E	E
C	Y	S	R	E	O	N	A	C
L	E	H	M	M	N	D	D	R
E	N	Y	T	E	E	L	E	I
I	A	L	I	G	N	M	B	M
H	E	I	G	H	T	U	G	E

align	bright	crime	cyclone	grind	height
hyena	knife	shy	sprite	tile	whine

2. Write a word that rhymes with the word below. The word does not have to be spelled the same to rhyme.

   a) whine _____ b) strike _____ c) rye _____

   d) style _____ e) flight _____ f) glide _____

Say each word out loud. Look at the different letters that make the long **o** sound.

Copy and spell each word three times using colours of your choice.

1. roam _____ _____ _____

2. poem _____ _____ _____

3. ratio _____ _____ _____

4. envelope _____ _____ _____

5. solar _____ _____ _____

6. owner _____ _____ _____

7. quote _____ _____ _____

8. piano _____ _____ _____

9. poem _____ _____ _____

10. loaves _____ _____ _____

Spelling Tips: A long *o* sound can be made with

- letter **o** (*troll, bonus, go*)
- letters **oe** (*toe*)
- letters **oa** and **ow** (*goal, throw*)
- letter **o** followed by a **consonant + e** (*mole*)

| envelope | loaves | owner | piano | poem |
| quote | ratio | remote | roam | solar |

1. Fill in the blank using the best spelling word from the list.

a) There are four _____ of bread cooling on the counter.

b) The science lab is in a very _____ location in Antarctica.

c) We need to add water and oil at a _____ of 2:1.

d) Our neighbours had _____ panels installed on their roof.

e) I'm learning to play a song called "Heart and Soul" on the _____.

f) Mrs. Kim started the meeting with a _____ about doing your best.

g) The _____ of the cat we found was very happy to get her back.

h) Antelopes _____ across the grasslands in Africa.

i) When the mail came, Mom gave me an _____ with my name on it.

j) Tao wrote a _____ about his favourite season, which is fall.

Brain Stretch

How many spelling words can you fit into one sentence and still make sense? Give it a try!

1. Underline the words in the story that have a long **o** sound.

The Oak & the Reeds (An Aesop's Fable)

A Giant Oak stood near a brook in which grew some slender Reeds. When the wind blew, the great Oak stood proudly upright with its hundred arms uplifted to the sky. But the Reeds bowed low in the wind and sang a sad and mournful song.

"You have reason to complain," said the Oak. "The slightest breeze that ruffles the surface of the water makes you bow your heads, while I, the mighty Oak, stand upright and firm before the howling tempest."

"Do not worry about us," replied the Reeds. "The winds do not harm us. We bow before them and so we do not break. You, in all your pride and strength, have so far resisted their blows. But the end is coming."

As the Reeds spoke, a great hurricane rushed out of the north. The Oak stood proudly and fought against the storm, while the yielding Reeds bowed low. The wind redoubled in fury, and all at once the great tree fell, torn up by the roots, and lay among the pitying Reeds.

Moral: Better to yield [stop resisting] when it is folly [foolishness] to resist, than to resist stubbornly and be destroyed.

2. An **antonym** is a word that has the opposite meaning of another word.

Circle the antonym for the bolded word.

a) **remote**   close   far   b) **frozen**   thawed   solid

3. What does **flowed** mean in the sentence? Circle the correct definition.

Amy's red hair flowed over her shoulders.

moved at a steady pace   hung loosely and gracefully

Spelling Week 9 – Word Study

envelope	loaves	owner	piano	poem
quote	ratio	remote	roam	solar

1. Write the correct spelling word from the list to match the clue.

   a) To move about or travel aimlessly over a large area _____

   b) A piece of writing consisting of lines that usually rhyme _____

   c) A flat paper container with a sealable flap that is
   used to contain a letter or document _____

   d) The person who owns something specific _____

   e) A musical instrument with a keyboard, a wooden case,
   and metal strings that are struck by hammers _____

   f) Having to do with the Sun or energy from its rays _____

   g) Distant; far away _____

   h) A copy of, or to refer to, someone's exact words _____

   i) A relationship between two amounts _____

   j) Quantities of bread that are shaped and baked in one
   piece and usually sliced before being eaten _____

2. Do **not** use the spelling word list for this activity. Write 2 words that have the long **o**
   sound made by the following letters:

   a) oe _____   b) oa _____

   c) ow _____   d) o _____

Say each word out loud. Look at the different letters that make the long *u* sound.

Copy and spell each word three times using colours of your choice.

1. fuel _____ _____ _____

2. vacuum _____ _____ _____

3. ambulance _____ _____ _____

4. barbecue _____ _____ _____

5. interview _____ _____ _____

6. mute _____ _____ _____

7. immune _____ _____ _____

8. review _____ _____ _____

9. musician _____ _____ _____

10. mute _____ _____ _____

Spelling Tips: A long *u* sound can be made with

- letter *u* followed by a **consonant + e** (*reuse*)
- letter *u* followed by a **consonant + i** or *y* (*cupid, jury*)
- letters *ue* (*cue*)
- letters *ew* (*few, ewe*)

Spelling Week 10 – Words with a Long *u* Sound

ambulance	barbecue	fuel	immune	interview
musician	mute	rescue	review	vacuum

1. Fill in the blank using the best spelling word from the list.

a) After we get our tests back, we will _____ it as a class.

b) This Monday, we will have an _____ with a guest speaker.

c) Mom cooked hamburgers and hot dogs on the _____.

d) An _____ came to take our neighbour Ken to the hospital.

e) Once you catch a virus, you are then _____ to it.

f) Push the _____ button on the TV if someone wants to speak to you.

g) The local animal _____ is having a fundraiser this weekend.

h) It takes _____ to make cars, trucks, buses, and motorcycles run.

i) My uncle is a very good jazz _____. He plays the trumpet.

j) On the weekends, I help Dad _____ the whole house.

Brain Stretch

How many spelling words can you fit into one sentence and still make sense?
Give it a try!

Long vowels say their name! So when you say words with long vowels, you hear the letter names **A** (game), **E** (team), **I** (bite), **O** (goat), and **U** (use).

The long **u** should sound just like the word **you**. For example, the word **June** sounds like **Jyoune**. Other letter combinations, such as **ew**, **ue**, and a **consonant + e, i**, or **y**, can also make the long **u** sound. However, all of those letters, including **u** itself, can also make other sounds that do not sound like the word **you**.

1. Say the word out loud. Listen for sounds the letters make. Underline the words that have the long **u** sound.

a) rescue	cue	clue	flu	unite
b) true	university	grew	menu	yule
c) chew	music	argue	flew	true
d) rescue	view	blue	unique	grew

2. The word **pupil** can have two meanings.

   Write a sentence to show each meaning of the word **pupil**.

   _____

   _____

3. Write a sentence using the word **communicate**.

   _____

Spelling Week 10 – Word Study

1. Use the word list below to look for the words in the puzzle.

   Circle the word in the word search puzzle. Then cross out the word in the list.

U	N	I	C	Y	C	L	E	A
N	E	I	D	L	M	N	O	R
I	R	C	E	C	O	O	Z	G
Q	C	C	U	E	I	C	Y	U
U	X	W	U	U	E	L	J	E
E	U	I	E	P	T	Z	E	G
V	N	D	W	F	I	E	W	E
O	I	Y	E	W	T	D	E	H
I	T	R	E	U	S	E	L	J
R	E	S	C	U	E	U	G	Z

argue	cue	cupid	ewe	jewel	June
rescue	reuse	unicycle	unique	unite	yew

2. Just for fun, let's look at some other letter combinations and words that have a long *u* sound. The letter combinations include *oo*, *oe*, *ui*, and *ugh*. Say the words out loud. Use the pronunciation key to pronounce any words you don't know.

shoo and shoe [shyou]   manual [man-you-ull]   Hugh [hyou]

juice [jyouss]   ukulele [you-kuh-lay-lee]   ewe [you]

Spelling Week 11 – Words with *y* as Long *i* and Long *e* Sounds

Say each word out loud. Listen for the long *i* and long *e* sounds.

Copy and spell each word three times using colours of your choice.

1. hyphen _____ _____ _____

2. alchemy _____ _____ _____

3. injury _____ _____ _____

4. directory _____ _____ _____

5. deny _____ _____ _____

6. electricity _____ _____ _____

7. buyer _____ _____ _____

8. notify _____ _____ _____

9. poultry _____ _____ _____

10. reply _____ _____ _____

Brain Stretch

- Create a word search puzzle based on the spelling words.
- On a piece of paper, write a sentence using each spelling word.

alchemy	buyer	deny	directory	electricity
hyphen	injury	notify	poultry	reply

1. Fill in the blank using the best spelling word from the list.

a) Turkeys, chickens, ducks, and geese are called _____.

b) Many words contain a _____, including left-handed and well-being.

c) I got an email from my cousin today and I'm going to _____ now.

d) The store said they would _____ us when the package was sent.

e) My grandfather has an old knee _____ that hurts him when it rains.

f) My lamp and radio are both run on _____.

g) Aunt Amy works as a _____ for a clothing store in the mall.

h) Check the _____ in the building to locate the doctor's office.

i) The early form of chemistry was called _____.

j) If you ask her, Jean will _____ that she likes Michael.

Brain Stretch

How many spelling words can you fit into one sentence and still make sense? Give it a try!

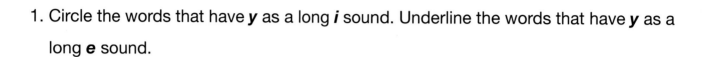

1. Circle the words that have **y** as a long **i** sound. Underline the words that have **y** as a long **e** sound.

   a) guy   many   plenty   display   cry

   b) smelly   replay   eventually   rely   recycle

   c) twenty   bylaw   carry   apply   royal

   d) prey   deny   alley   history   spy

   e) hungry   style   angry   rely   repay

   f) kayak   clay   verify   fairy   cherry

2. Circle the compound words. Write the two words that make the word with a **+** sign.

   Example: doghouse   *dog + house*

   a) haircut   deny   fly   nightmare   crayon

   _____

   b) cherry   nobody   monkey   apply   caveman

   _____

   c) dragonfly   strawberry   berry   firecracker   afraid

   _____

alchemy	buyer	deny	directory	electricity
hyphen	injury	notify	poultry	reply

1. Write the correct spelling word from the list to match the clue.

a) To inform someone of something, usually in a formal
or official manner   _____

b) An organized listing of individuals or organizations   _____

c) Refuse to admit something   _____

d) The medieval form of chemistry; the process of trying
to turn something ordinary, such as lead, into
something valuable, such as gold   _____

e) Harm or damage caused   _____

f) Respond to something that was said or done   _____

g) Someone who buys goods, usually for a store to sell   _____

h) Domestic fowl such as chickens, turkeys, ducks, and
geese   _____

i) A form of energy resulting from charged particles   _____

j) A sign used to join words to indicate that they have
a combined meaning   _____

2. The word *type* can have two meanings. Write a sentence to show each meaning.

_____

_____

Say each word out loud. Think about what letter or letters are missing.

Copy and spell each word three times using colours of your choice.

1. it's _____ _____ _____

2. he'll _____ _____ _____

3. you're _____ _____ _____

4. couldn't _____ _____ _____

5. I've _____ _____ _____

6. they'll _____ _____ _____

7. haven't _____ _____ _____

8. we've _____ _____ _____

9. won't _____ _____ _____

10. she'd _____ _____ _____

Brain Stretch

- Create a word search puzzle based on the spelling words.
- On a piece of paper, write a sentence using each spelling word.

Spelling Week 12 – Contractions

couldn't	haven't	he'll	it's	I've
she'd	they'll	we've	won't	you're

1. Fill in the blank using the best spelling word from the list.

a) Becky said _____ like to have a bologna sandwich for lunch today.

b) Mom and Dad said _____ take us to the zoo tomorrow.

c) _____ been studying for the test for a whole week.

d) The store clerk said he _____ find the cereal we wanted.

e) If we're going to get to the movie on time, _____ got to leave now.

f) Ted _____ stop climbing until he falls out of a tree and hurts himself.

g) I heard that _____ going to Alberta on your vacation next month.

h) The baby rat was so cute, I _____ leave him at the pet store.

i) I _____ been to the library in months.

j) Dad said _____ mow the lawn this afternoon, then we can play catch.

Brain Stretch

How many spelling words can you fit into one sentence and still make sense?
Give it a try!

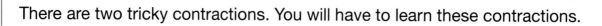

Spelling Week 12 – Word Study

There are two tricky contractions. You will have to learn these contractions.

will not = won't   **cannot = can't**

1. Circle the incorrect contraction. Write the correct contraction at the end of the sentence.

a) Marco willn't be coming swimming this weekend. _____

b) I cann't wait for school to start again! _____

c) Sara wil'nt tell May's secret to anyone. _____

d) Jon cant see clearly without his glasses. _____

e) Donot you want to go for a walk with us? _____

f) Hasnot she seen this movie before? _____

2. Read the contraction. Write the words in full.

Example: I'm   I am

a) couldn't _____   b) hasn't _____

c) we're _____   d) she'd _____

e) that's _____   f) don't _____

g) can't _____   h) won't _____

i) you'll _____   j) he's _____

48   © Chalkboard Publishing Inc

1. Using the word list below, write all the contractions for the full word.

I you he she it they we he she

Full Word	Contractions
are	
am	
will	
has or is	
would or had	
have	

2. Read the words in the brackets. Make a contraction from those words and write it on the line.

a) Terry _____ find his favourite socks to wear to school. (could not)

b) Penny _____ happy about how her project turned out. (was not)

c) Kent _____ had a cold in many years. (has not)

d) Afnan _____ eat her carrots tonight. (will not)

e) Kelly _____ touch her toes because she hurt her back. (cannot)

f) Jay _____ talk so loudly in the library. (should not)

Spelling Week 13 – Double Consonants

Say each word out loud. Watch for the double consonants.

Copy and spell each word three times using colours of your choice.

1. happiness _____ _____ _____

2. common _____ _____ _____

3. immediately _____ _____ _____

4. appreciate _____ _____ _____

5. dessert _____ _____ _____

6. forgetting _____ _____ _____

7. crystallize _____ _____ _____

8. manner _____ _____ _____

9. discuss _____ _____ _____

10. marriage _____ _____ _____

Brain Stretch

- Create a word search puzzle based on the spelling words.
- On a piece of paper, write a sentence using each spelling word.

appreciate	common	crystallize	dessert	discuss
forgetting	happiness	immediately	manner	marriage

1. Fill in the blank using the best spelling word from the list.

a) I keep _____ to brush my teeth after meals, so Dad reminds me.

b) Intense heat and pressure causes carbon to _____ into diamonds.

c) I really _____ it when Mom helps me with my math homework.

d) Our cat purrs with _____ when someone pats or scratches her.

e) In class today, we got into groups to _____ children's rights.

f) When the fire drill happens, we must _____ line up to go outside.

g) After dinner tonight, we're having ice cream for _____.

h) Last weekend, my whole family went to a fancy _____ ceremony.

i) Our cat is a tabby, which is a very _____ breed.

j) I need to arrange my science project in a very interesting _____.

Brain Stretch

How many spelling words can you fit into one sentence and still make sense?
Give it a try!

Spelling Week 13 – Word Study

For many verbs that end with **consonant + vowel + consonant**, double the final consonant before adding *ed* or *ing*.

Examples:	**Verb**	**Add ed**	**Add ing**
	fan	*fanned*	*fanning*
	snap	*snapped*	*snapping*

1. Add *ed* and *ing* to the verb. Remember to double the final consonant when needed.

a) fuss _____ _____

b) knit _____ _____

c) shrug _____ _____

d) plant _____ _____

e) travel _____ _____

2. Put a ✔ beside the word if it is spelled correctly. If the word is spelled incorrectly, put an **X** beside the word and write the word correctly.

a) glowwing _____   b) fainted _____

c) skipped _____   d) mashhing _____

e) marveled _____   f) sweatting _____

g) coughed _____   h) talkking _____

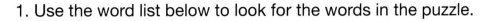

1. Use the word list below to look for the words in the puzzle.

   Circle the word in the word search puzzle. Then cross out the word in the list.

A	P	P	R	O	V	A	L	S
B	E	L	I	T	T	L	E	C
P	O	T	T	E	R	N	P	R
U	Z	P	I	Z	Z	A	P	I
D	I	N	N	E	R	A	Y	B
D	P	F	Y	S	T	E	D	B
L	P	D	O	L	L	A	R	L
E	E	B	U	T	T	O	N	E
S	R	A	C	C	O	O	N	M
C	H	A	L	L	E	N	G	E

approval	belittle	button	challenge	dinner	dollar
otter	pizza	puddle	raccoon	scribble	zipper

2. Write a word that rhymes with the word below. The words do not have to be spelled the same.

a) small _____   b) critter _____   c) chill _____

d) platter _____   e) boss _____   f) clutter _____

g) sunny _____   h) shell _____   i) missed _____

Say each word out loud. Listen for which letters you don't hear.

Copy and spell each word three times using colours of your choice.

1. league _____ _____ _____

2. daylight _____ _____ _____

3. athlete _____ _____ _____

4. rehearse _____ _____ _____

5. descent _____ _____ _____

6. autumn _____ _____ _____

7. knead _____ _____ _____

8. cologne _____ _____ _____

9. wrinkle _____ _____ _____

10. salmon _____ _____ _____

Spelling Tip

For many words that end in a vowel followed by a **consonant + silent e**, the **e** makes the vowel say its name.

athlete	autumn	cologne	daylight	descent
knead	league	rehearse	salmon	wrinkle

1. Fill in the blank using the best spelling word from the list.

a) My Aunt Jackie belongs to a women's roller derby _____.

b) In spring and summer, birds start to sing long before it is _____.

c) I have to stand up as much as possible so I don't _____ my dress.

d) Our first performance is tomorrow night, so we need _____ today.

e) In _____, leaves change colour and fall off the trees.

f) Jack wears very strong _____ that makes me sneeze.

g) My sister was an _____ in school. She competed in the high jump.

h) Firefighters made a rope _____ into the cave to find the lost boy.

i) In British Columbia, bears have a feast when the _____ migrate.

j) Dad has me help him _____ the bread so it will rise properly.

Brain Stretch

How many spelling words can you fit into one sentence and still make sense?
Give it a try!

Spelling Week 14 – Word Study

1. Say the word out loud. Can you hear all the letter sounds? Circle words with silent letters. Underline the silent letters.

a) anchor   honest   scoop   storm   raspberry

b) ballet   design   yellow   menu   fasten

c) chemical   clump   guard   crew   debris

d) books   review   answer   science   bristles

e) people   gnome   plumber   shook   tongue

2. Say the word out loud. Add **e** to the end of the word. Write the new word. Say the word again. Even though the **e** is silent, it still changes the way the vowel sounds.

	Add **e**		Add **e**
a) sham		b) grad	
c) scar		d) cut	
e) rob		f) scrap	
g) grim		h) plan	

3. What happens to the vowel when you add **e** to the end of the word?

_____

4. Say the word out loud. Write **L** if the vowel has a long sound or **S** if it has a short sound.

a) share ___   b) glitter ___   c) bright ___   d) brain ___

e) traction ___   f) stay ___   g) honey ___   h) shale ___

Spelling Week 14 – Word Study

athlete	autumn	cologne	daylight	descent
knead	league	rehearse	salmon	wrinkle

1. Write the correct spelling word from the list to match the clue.

a) To work something with the hands to form a dough   _____

b) A large edible fish with reddish or pinkish flesh   _____

c) An association of people or groups with common

   interests or goals   _____

d) The natural light of day; dawn   _____

e) To practice something for later public performance   _____

f) Season in which leaves change colour and fall off trees   _____

g) A slight line or fold in something, such as fabric or skin on

   the face; make or cause lines or folds in fabric or skin   _____

h) A person who is skilled in sports   _____

i) Action of moving, dropping, or falling downward   _____

j) A perfumed liquid to put on the skin   _____

2. Do **not** use the spelling word list for this activity. Write a word that has the following

   silent letters:

a) wr _____   b) gh _____

c) b _____   d) t _____

Say each word out loud. Look at the different letters that make long and short *oo* sounds. Copy and spell each word three times using colours of your choice.

1. raccoon _____ _____ _____

2. notebook _____ _____ _____

3. bookshelf _____ _____ _____

4. outlook _____ _____ _____

5. kangaroo _____ _____ _____

6. smoothie _____ _____ _____

7. foolish _____ _____ _____

8. shampoo _____ _____ _____

9. wooden _____ _____ _____

10. footstool _____ _____ _____

Spelling Tips

The long *oo* sound can be spelled with
- letters *ew* (*drew*) and *ue* (*blue*)
- letters *oo* (*baboon*)
- letters *ough* (*through*)

The short *oo* sound can be spelled with
- letters *oo* (*shook*)
- letters *ou* (*would*)

Spelling Week 15 – Words with Long and Short *oo* Sounds

bookshelf	**foolish**	**footstool**	**kangaroo**	**notebook**
outlook	**raccoon**	**shampoo**	**smoothie**	**wooden**

1. Fill in the blank using the best spelling word from the list.

a) Dad made me a strawberry and banana _____ for breakfast.

b) The happiest people have a positive _____ on life.

c) I have a _____ that has animal pictures all over the cover.

d) Grandma keeps photos of me and my family on her _____.

e) The mother _____ carries her baby in her pouch until it is bigger.

f) We have a _____ family living in our attic!

g) The farmer was _____ when he killed the goose for her golden eggs.

h) My favourite _____ smells like fresh lemon juice.

i) That house has a huge, curving _____ staircase in the front hall.

j) Fluffy often curls up to sleep on the _____ by the sunny window.

Brain Stretch

How many spelling words can you fit into one sentence and still make sense?
Give it a try!

1. Circle the words that have a long **oo** sound. Some of the words have the same sound but are spelled differently.

a) wood	tuna	tough	crew	glue
b) route	dune	shoulder	cloud	fruit
c) plume	grumpy	noodle	hours	renew
d) hooks	spruce	soup	scuba	enough

2. Circle the words that have a short **oo** sound. Some of the words have the same sound but are spelled differently.

a) pudding	gold	should	flu	woman
b) mole	wool	threw	puss	fulcrum
c) cookie	caboose	sugar	blew	bull
d) push	view	butcher	brook	octopus

3. Write the correct letter beside the word. Write **S** for a short **oo** sound, **L** for a long **oo** sound, and **N** for neither sound.

a) pulley _____   b) cuff _____   c) spoon _____

d) crown _____   e) suit _____   f) bushel _____

g) tongue _____   h) hoodie _____   i) tuba _____

1. Use the word list below to look for the words in the puzzle.

   Circle the word in the word search puzzle. Then cross out the word in the list.

T	C	R	U	E	L	J	B	K
F	O	O	T	P	R	I	N	T
B	O	G	S	R	W	G	S	X
O	K	H	H	F	I	O	P	B
O	I	O	O	D	V	O	O	R
K	E	U	O	S	T	D	O	O
L	R	L	K	O	T	B	L	O
E	W	O	U	L	D	Y	I	M
T	O	O	L	S	D	E	B	J
B	P	Y	W	L	O	O	T	Z

booklet	broom	cookie	cruel	footprint	ghoul
goodbye	loot	spool	tools	shook	would

2. Write a word that rhymes with the word below. Rhyming words do not have to be

   spelled in the same way.

   a) brute _____   b) brook _____   c) spoon _____

   d) doom _____   e) pull _____   f) brew _____

   g) cruel _____   h) should _____   i) juice _____

Spelling Week 16 – Words with *oi* and *oy*

Say each word out loud. Listen to the sounds *oi* and *oy* make.

Copy and spell each word three times using colours of your choice.

1. oysters _____ _____ _____

2. choice _____ _____ _____

3. cowboy _____ _____ _____

4. spoiled _____ _____ _____

5. destroy _____ _____ _____

6. asteroid _____ _____ _____

7. voyage _____ _____ _____

8. gargoyle _____ _____ _____

9. noisy _____ _____ _____

10. coiled _____ _____ _____

Brain Stretch

- Create a word search puzzle based on the spelling words.
- On a piece of paper, write a sentence using each spelling word.

asteroid   **choice**   **coiled**   **cowboy**   **destroy**

gargoyle   **noisy**   **oysters**   **spoiled**   **voyage**

1. Fill in the blank using the best spelling word from the list.

a) A dog in the neighbour is very _____. He never stops barking!

b) The _____ belt is a region between the orbits of Jupiter and Mars.

c) Our teacher gave us the _____ of painting or collages today.

d) My brother accidentally left the milk on the counter and it _____.

e) The big snake sat _____ like a rope near the rocks.

f) Aunt Lucy took a very long sea _____ from here to Italy.

g) My uncle is a _____ who competes in the Calgary Stampede.

h) The old church has a big _____ statue at each corner of the roof.

i) I like the smell of smoked _____, but I don't like to eat them.

j) My pet rat Winston likes to _____ his blankets and wooden toys.

Brain Stretch

How many spelling words can you fit into one sentence and still make sense?
Give it a try!

1. Read the sentence clue. Unscramble the spelling word and write it in the space.

a) In many places, a man can still find work as a _____. (wbocyo)

b) We must be kind and not be _____ when someone is sleeping. (soniy)

c) My favourite part of old buildings is the _____. (lgyragoe)

d) When given the _____, I would rather participate than observe. (ohicec)

e) A forest fire will _____ every living thing in its path. (odteyrs)

f) Did you know _____ move by crawling on the ocean floor? (rotyses)

g) If you pat the dog every time he asks, he will get _____. (ldposie)

2. Write a compound word using the given word.

a) _____ball   b) brain_____

c) book_____   d) _____box

e) _____ship   f) some_____

g) _____fly   h) bed_____

i) sun_____   j) _____self

k) fire_____   l) eye_____

Spelling Week 16 – Word Study

asteroid	**choice**	**coiled**	**cowboy**	**destroy**
gargoyle	**noisy**	**oysters**	**spoiled**	**voyage**

1. Write the correct spelling word from the list to match the clue.

a) Unfit for eating; harmed the character of someone by
   being too permissive and indulgent   _____

b) Molluscs that have a rough shell and can produce pearls _____

c) A small rocky body that orbits the Sun   _____

d) Making a lot of loud or unpleasant noise   _____

e) A man on horseback who tends and herds cattle   _____

f) A long journey by sea or in space   _____

g) The act of selecting or make a decision when faced
   with two or more possibilities   _____

h) To put an end to the existence of something   _____

i) A grotesque carved face or figure projecting from the
   gutter of a building, usually for carrying rainwater _____

j) Arranged in a continuous series of spirals, one above
   or inside the other   _____

2. Do **not** use the spelling word list for this activity. Write four words that contain the

   following letters:

   a) oi _____

   b) oy _____

Say each word out loud. Listen for the **ow** sound. Copy and spell each word three times using colours of your choice.

1. flounder   _____ _____ _____

2. discount   _____ _____ _____

3. chowder   _____ _____ _____

4. announce   _____ _____ _____

5. drowsy   _____ _____ _____

6. trowel   _____ _____ _____

7. surrounded   _____ _____ _____

8. downspout   _____ _____ _____

9. thousand   _____ _____ _____

10. shower   _____ _____ _____

Brain Stretch

- Create a word search puzzle based on the spelling words.
- On a piece of paper, write a sentence using each spelling word.

| announce | chowder | discount | downspout | drowsy |
| flounder | shower | surrounded | thousand | trowel |

1. Fill in the blank using the best spelling word from the list.

a) Mom and I both use our own _____ to dig in the garden.

b) After your _____, we can braid your wet hair to make it wavy.

c) A chipmunk keeps hiding in the _____ at the corner of the house.

d) A millennium is a period of one _____ years.

e) The medicine Dad is taking makes him _____ so he can't drive.

f) Today, the mayor will _____ plans for a new commuter train.

g) A _____ is a flat fish that has both eyes on the same side of its head.

h) Grandma is making her famous clam _____ for our dinner.

i) We bought our new television at a very good _____.

j) An island is a body of land that is completely _____ by water.

Brain Stretch

How many spelling words can you fit into one sentence and still make sense?
Give it a try!

1. The letters **ou** and **ow** can have an **ow** sound or an **o** sound. Say the word out loud. Underline the words that have an **ow** sound. Circle the words that have an **o** sound.

a) plough	crowd	although	allow	glow
b) shout	tomorrow	aloud	narrow	borrow
c) slouch	sparrow	scowl	snowball	trout
d) bounce	throw	fountain	tower	shallow

2. **Homophones** are words that sound the same, but are spelled differently and have different meanings. Say the word out loud. Draw a line from the word to its meaning.

a) sweet   use carelessly or for no reason; discarded materials

b) suite   part of the human body between the ribs and hips

c) yolk   mixture of gases living things need to live

d) yoke   person entitled to inherit specific property

e) air   set of rooms for an individual's or family's use, or for a particular purpose

f) heir   yellow internal part of an animal's or bird's egg

g) waist   pleasant taste similar to sugar or honey

h) waste   wooden crosspiece fastened over the necks of two animals and attached to a cart or plough for pulling

Spelling Week 17 – Word Study

1. Use the word list below to look for the words in the puzzle.

   Circle the word in the word search puzzle. Then cross out the word in the list.

F	O	U	N	T	A	I	N	S
A	B	I	G	R	O	U	C	H
L	O	H	O	U	R	O	Z	A
L	R	J	S	F	I	I	Y	L
O	R	C	N	Q	A	T	T	L
W	O	S	O	U	T	H	O	O
V	W	Y	W	F	G	F	W	W
O	Y	A	C	O	L	L	E	H
P	O	U	C	H	O	M	R	J
M	A	R	R	O	W	U	G	Z

allow	borrow	fountain	glow	grouch	hour
marrow	pouch	shallow	snow	south	tower

2. Write a word ending in the same letters underlined below. Words don't have to rhyme.

Examples: **p<u>out</u>**   **sc<u>out</u>**   **<u>down</u>**   **<u>gown</u>**   **c<u>ount</u>**   **m<u>ount</u>**

a) fa<u>llow</u> _____

b) cr<u>own</u> _____

c) h<u>our</u> _____

d) gr<u>owl</u> _____

e) h<u>ound</u> _____

f) sh<u>ower</u> _____

g) s<u>outh</u> _____

h) cl<u>oud</u> _____

i) gr<u>ouse</u> _____

Say each word out loud. Look at the different letters that make an *s* sound. Copy and spell each word three times using colours of your choice.

1. entrance _____ _____ _____

2. saucer _____ _____ _____

3. exciting _____ _____ _____

4. crystal _____ _____ _____

5. possible _____ _____ _____

6. earliest _____ _____ _____

7. instead _____ _____ _____

8. juicy _____ _____ _____

9. promise _____ _____ _____

10. exciting _____ _____ _____

Spelling Tip

The *s* sound can be spelled with the letters *s*, *ce*, *ci*, and *cy*.

crystal	earliest	entrance	exciting	instead
juicy	possible	promise	saucer	scissors

1. Fill in the blank using the best spelling word from the list.

a) This ripe peach is incredibly sweet and _____!

b) Mr. Kim asked if it was _____ for me to walk his dog every day.

c) I made a _____ to myself that I would always try very hard to be kind.

d) I found a dress I liked in blue, but I'd rather have purple _____.

e) It's hard to balance a cup of tea on a _____ while walking.

f) Tiffany found a beautiful rose quartz _____ on the beach.

g) It's so _____ to think that our play is opening next Tuesday!

h) The _____ Dad could get in to see the doctor is next Friday.

i) Han stood at the _____ to the library waiting for Theo to arrive.

j) Mom gets mad if we use her fabric _____ to cut paper or hair.

Brain Stretch

How many spelling words can you fit into one sentence and still make sense? Give it a try!

1. Say the word out loud. Circle the words that do **not** have an *s* sound.

a)	phrase	organism	pastel	piece	measure
b)	cousin	fleece	dessert	receive	wisdom
c)	business	clothes	mercy	vision	canvas
d)	cheese	raise	recite	poison	since

2. *Homographs* are words that are spelled the same, but have different meanings and can sometimes sound different. Read the pronunciation key if there is one. Draw a line from the word to its meaning. You can use a dictionary, if needed.

a) close [KLOHss]	poor reason for having done something
b) close [KLOHz]	injury in which the skin is cut or broken
c) object [OBjekt]	to lessen the blame for something
d) object [obJEKT]	shut something
e) excuse [ex-KYOOS]	material thing that can be seen and touched
f) excuse [ex-KYOOZ]	repeatedly twisted or coiled something around itself or a core; turned a key repeatedly to make a clock, watch, or clockwork object operate
g) wound [WOOnd]	nearby
h) wound [WOWnd]	say something to express disapproval or disagreement with something

1. Use the word list below to look for the words in the puzzle.

   Circle the word in the word search puzzle. Then cross out the word in the list.

W	C	O	N	D	E	N	S	E
H	I	R	E	C	I	P	E	P
I	R	P	L	V	P	K	Q	R
S	C	E	C	P	U	M	U	I
T	U	A	E	T	R	E	I	V
L	I	C	T	F	P	S	N	A
E	T	E	F	L	O	S	S	C
O	Y	X	P	B	S	A	W	Y
G	L	A	N	C	E	G	B	J
S	P	I	C	Y	H	E	G	Z

circuit	condense	floss	glance	message	peace
privacy	purpose	recipe	sequins	spicy	whistle

2. Write a word that rhymes with the word below. They can be spelled differently.

a) swift _____   b) slice _____   c) dance _____

d) wrist _____   e) chase _____   f) guess _____

g) vest _____   h) spruce _____   i) spider _____

Say each word out loud. Look at the different letters that make a *j* sound.

Copy and spell each word three times using colours of your choice.

1. sponge   _____   _____   _____

2. allergy   _____   _____   _____

3. judge   _____   _____   _____

4. contagious   _____   _____   _____

5. strategy   _____   _____   _____

6. gigantic   _____   _____   _____

7. imaginary   _____   _____   _____

8. junior   _____   _____   _____

9. jacket   _____   _____   _____

10. manager   _____   _____   _____

Spelling Tip

The *j* sound can be spelled with the letters *j*, *ge*, *gy*, and *gi*.

allergy	contagious	gigantic	imaginary	jacket
judge	junior	manager	sponge	strategy

1. Fill in the blank using the best spelling word from the list.

a) My brother is in the _____ A hockey league in Toronto.

b) It's very chilly outside today. I think I will wear my _____.

c) Every person in my family has at least one type of _____.

d) The spider's main _____ was to catch the fly so he could wrap it up.

e) The people have to taste the pies and _____ which is the best.

f) The equator is an _____ line around the centre of Earth.

g) About a week after catching a cold, you are no longer _____.

h) Aunt Zara is the _____ at the big flower shop in the city.

i) I get to use a big _____ when I help my sister wash the car.

j) Grandad grew one _____ pumpkin to enter in the fall fair.

Brain Stretch

How many spelling words can you fit into one sentence and still make sense?
Give it a try!

1. Say the word out loud. Circle the words that do **not** have a *j* sound.

a) angle   angel   girl   jewellery   giant

b) injury   gymnastics   organic   pigeon   ringer

c) gentle   janitor   gardener   fridge   guard

d) magician   geese   wriggle   range   ginger

2. The letters "ology" mean "the study of." When these letters are added to the end of a word, the beginning of the word tells what is being studied. Use your knowledge or the Internet to find an "ology" you are interested in. Write a paragraph describing what the word means, what is being studied, and what the study involves.

_____

_____

_____

_____

_____

_____

_____

allergy	contagious	gigantic	imaginary	jacket
judge	junior	manager	sponge	strategy

1. Write the correct spelling word from the list to match the clue.

   a) Soft material full of holes, used for absorbing liquids _____

   b) Low or lower in rank or status _____

   c) The body's damaging immune response to a substance
      to which is has become excessively sensitive _____

   d) Existing only in one's imagination _____

   e) Person in charge of controlling or running all or part of
      a business or an organization _____

   f) Of very great size or extent; huge or enormous _____

   g) Spread from one person or organism to another
      through direct or indirect contact _____

   h) Form an opinion or draw a conclusion about something _____

   i) Plan of action designed to achieve a specific aim or goal _____

   j) An outer garment that extends to the waist or hips, has
      sleeves, and fastens down the front _____

2. Do **not** use the spelling word list for this activity. Write a word that has the *j* sound made
   by the following letters. These letters can be anywhere in the word.

   a) j _____ b) ge _____

   c) gi _____ d) gy _____

Say each word out loud. Listen to the *f* sound the different letters make.

Copy and spell each word three times using colours of your choice.

1. trophies   _____   _____   _____

2. relief   _____   _____   _____

3. prefer   _____   _____   _____

4. telephone   _____   _____   _____

5. cough   _____   _____   _____

6. enough   _____   _____   _____

7. safety   _____   _____   _____

8. elephant   _____   _____   _____

9. physical   _____   _____   _____

10. tough   _____   _____   _____

Brain Stretch

- Create a word search puzzle based on the spelling words.
- On a piece of paper, write a sentence using each spelling word.

| cough | elephant | enough | physical | prefer |
| relief | safety | telephone | tough | trophies |

1. Fill in the blank using the best spelling word from the list.

a) It was such a _____ to finally arrive home before the big storm hit.

b) Mom taught all of us how to dial 911 on the _____ at a young age.

c) _____ is the most important thing when riding a bicycle.

d) We have just _____ flour to make one batch of banana muffins.

e) Cousin Tom has a lot of _____ from track-and-field competitions.

f) My favourite animal is the gigantic African _____.

g) Every time I have a cold, I still have the _____ long after it's over.

h) Janet is very excited about teaching _____ fitness classes.

i) I like warm hoodies, but I _____ my purple-and-green sweater.

j) The apples have very _____ skins this year.

Brain Stretch

How many spelling words can you fit into one sentence and still make sense?
Give it a try!

A **metaphor** is a figure of speech that compares two things that are not alike but have something in common. Metaphors compare by saying something **is** something else. Metaphors do **not** use the words **like** or **as** to compare.

*Example: The stars **are** sparkling diamonds in the night sky.*

1. Write a metaphor to complete the sentence. Remember not to use **like** or **as**.

   a) My toes are _____ when I play in the snow.

   b) The sun is a _____ in the evening sky.

   c) Freshy baked bread is _____ to my nose.

   d) My bedroom is a _____ when I'm feeling sad.

   e) Gently falling snowflakes are _____.

   f) The stormy sea is _____.

   g) Thunder is _____.

2. A **synonym** is a word that means the same as another word. Circle the synonym for the bolded word.

   a) **enough**   done   plenty   b) **relief**   calmness   excitement

3. An **antonym** is a word that has the opposite meaning of another word. Circle the antonym for the bolded word.

   a) **safety**   confidence   danger   b) **phony**   fake   genuine

1. Use the word list below to look for the words in the puzzle.

   Circle the word in the word search puzzle. Then cross out the word in the list.

S	T	U	F	F	I	N	G	F
A	P	H	I	D	M	N	O	A
K	H	Y	P	H	E	N	P	B
M	O	F	M	D	T	S	H	U
U	N	L	A	U	G	H	E	L
F	E	O	M	W	T	X	R	O
F	L	U	F	F	Y	D	F	U
L	Y	P	H	O	T	O	I	S
E	N	Y	M	P	H	M	S	J
R	T	R	O	U	G	H	G	Z

aphid	fabulous	fluffy	gopher	hyphen	laugh
muffler	nymph	phone	photo	trough	stuffing

2. Write a word that rhymes with the word below. The word doesn't have to be spelled the same.

   a) graph _____   b) stuff _____   c) rake _____

   d) seal _____   e) fudge _____   f) phone _____

   g) sphinx _____   h) finch _____   i) file _____

Spelling Week 21 – Consonant Digraphs: *ch, sh, th,* and *wh*

Say each word out loud. Listen for the different sounds the digraphs make.

Copy and spell each word three times using colours of your choice.

1. shampoo

2. myth

3. strength

4. character

5. whether

6. exchange

7. shelves

8. establish

9. whose

10. theme

Brain Stretch

- Create a word search puzzle based on the spelling words.
- On a piece of paper, write a sentence using each spelling word.

character	establish	exchange	mythology	shampoo
shelves	strength	theme	whether	whose

1. Fill in the blank using the best spelling word from the list.

a)   Hercules was a mythological character who had great _____.

b)   Arnie will be a ghost for Halloween and I will be a comic _____.

c)   The story about Jason and the Argonauts is from Greek _____.

d)   Ants work hard to _____ a large working colony underground.

e)   Dad is building some _____ for Mom to put her plants on.

f)   My aunt gave me pants that are too small so I have to _____ them.

g)   The party's _____ was the circus. We all dressed up as clowns!

h)   My favourite _____ smells like fresh lemons.

i)   Uncle Peter asked _____ we wanted a burger or a hot dog.

j)   Mom asked, "_____ mess is this? Come and clean it up!"

Brain Stretch

How many spelling words can you fit into one sentence and still make sense? Give it a try!

Spelling Week 21 – Word Study

1. Write the correct digraph letters in the word. Use **ch**, **sh**, **th**, or **wh**. Say the word out loud to check it.

   a) bun_____   b) _____ought   c) _____ingles   d) six_____

   e) di_____   f) _____urch   g) _____roat   h) _____ole

   i) _____ing   j) _____isper   k) squa_____   l) _____eck

2. How many words can you make? Use only **ch, sh, th,** and **wh** and the letters given to make the words. Say the word out loud to make sure it's a real word. Write your words on the line.

   Examples: am   wham   sham

   a) ip _____

   b) ick _____

   c) wi _____

   d) at _____

   e) en _____

   f) in _____

   g) eat _____

   h) ose _____

character	establish	exchange	mythology	shampoo
shelves	strength	theme	whether	whose

1. Write the correct spelling word from the list to match the clue.

a) Quality or state of being physically strong   _____

b) Give something and receive something of the same
   kind or value in return   _____

c) Flat lengths of wood or other rigid material that provide
   a surface for the storage or display of objects   _____

d) A word that expresses a doubt or a choice between
   alternatives   _____

e) Set up a business or organization on a firm or
   permanent foundation; give something a good start   _____

f) A collection of myths, especially one belonging to a
   particular cultural or religious tradition   _____

g) Subject, topic, or message in a story or talk; specific
   setting or atmosphere for a party or activity   _____

h) Liquid preparation containing detergent or soap for
   washing hair   _____

i) Word that questions which person or living being
   something belongs to or is associated with   _____

j) Person or other living being in a play, novel, or movie   _____

Say each word out loud. Listen to the sounds each consonant blend makes.

Copy and spell each word three times using colours of your choice.

1. instruction _____ _____ _____

2. splinter _____ _____ _____

3. sprained _____ _____ _____

4. struggle _____ _____ _____

5. splatters _____ _____ _____

6. sprinkle _____ _____ _____

7. screech _____ _____ _____

8. display _____ _____ _____

9. screen _____ _____ _____

10. strive _____ _____ _____

Brain Stretch

- Create a word search puzzle based on the spelling words.
- On a piece of paper, write a sentence using each spelling word.

Spelling Week 22 – Consonant Blends: *scr, spl, spr,* and *str*

display	instruction	screech	screen	splatters
splice	sprained	sprinkle	strive	struggle

1. Fill in the blank using the best spelling word from the list.

a) Every day, I _____ to be a better person than I was the day before.

b) Puppies tend to _____ a lot when you pick them up.

c) The gulls _____ when they think another gull might take their food.

d) Our teacher wants to _____ all of our projects for guests to look at.

e) Kenny can cut and _____ film to connect two parts of a movie.

f) Talia _____ her ankle when she slipped down a hill while hiking.

g) We need to read the _____ sheet to put together the bookcase.

h) My sister's dog opens the _____ door when he wants to go out.

i) The pack says to _____ the seeds with water daily till they sprout.

j) When my little brother waters the garden, mud _____ all over him.

Brain Stretch

How many spelling words can you fit into one sentence and still make sense?
Give it a try!

Write a short story using as many of these new words as you can.

bedspread	**bistro**	**ostrich**	**script**	**scrubbed**
splat	**sprite**	**spritz**	**streak**	**sunscreen**

_____

_____

_____

_____

_____

_____

_____

_____

_____

1. Use the word list below to look for the words in the puzzle.

   Circle the word in the puzzle. Then cross out the word in the list.

S	C	R	I	B	B	L	E	N
P	O	S	T	R	I	C	H	K
L	K	E	S	T	R	E	L	M
U	S	C	R	I	M	P	T	I
R	P	B	I	S	T	R	O	S
G	S	T	R	E	A	K	E	P
E	O	S	P	R	I	T	E	R
E	S	P	R	I	T	Z	F	I
S	U	N	S	C	R	E	E	N
C	O	N	S	T	R	U	C	T

bistro	construct	kestrel	misprint	ostrich	scribble
scrimp	splurge	sprite	spritz	streak	sunscreen

2. Write **scr, spl, spr,** or **str** to make a word. Make sure to say the word out loud to

   check it.

   a) _____unch   b) _____eet   c) _____itz

   d) _____eam   e) _____ub   f) _____at

   g) _____ipt   h) _____ayer   i) _____ength

   j) _____out   k) _____ipes   l) _____ead

When the letter *r* follows a vowel, it changes the sound of the vowel.

Examples: cat car   box born   gift girl   vet verb   cut curl

Say each word out loud. Listen to how the vowels are pronounced. Copy and spell each word three times using colours of your choice.

1. earthworm _____ _____ _____

2. inspire _____ _____ _____

3. dormitory _____ _____ _____

4. require _____ _____ _____

5. search _____ _____ _____

6. purchase _____ _____ _____

7. emergency _____ _____ _____

8. desert _____ _____ _____

9. enormous _____ _____ _____

10. occurs _____ _____ _____

| desert | dormitory | earthworm | emergency | enormous |
| inspire | occurs | purchase | require | search |

1. Fill in the blank using the best spelling word from the list.

a) My grandfather is trying to _____ a dark-purple amethyst crystal.

b) Katy lives in a _____ on the university campus where she studies.

c) There's an _____ spider web attached to the deck railing!

d) When I have a project to do, I _____ the Internet for information.

e) Seeing the things artistic people make can _____ others to create.

f) Scorpions, lizards, and rabbits are just some of the _____ animals.

g) An _____ makes air pockets in soil, which helps roots breathe.

h) When an accident happens, _____ crews get to work on it quickly.

i) A full moon _____ roughly every 29.5 days.

j) Some flower bulbs _____ extra protection from the winter cold.

Brain Stretch

How many spelling words can you fit into one sentence and still make sense? Give it a try!

The letter combinations listed below all make an *er* sound, however, that's not always true. The same letter combination can make different sounds. For example, in the word **work**, the *or* as an *er* sound, but in the word **pork** it does not. Also, when a vowel is followed by a **consonant + e, i,** or **y**, the vowel usually says its name (*a, e, i, o,* or *u*). When that happens, the same combination of letters don't have an *er* sound, such as in the words **her** and **here**.

1. Write a word with an *er* sound made by the given letters. Then write a word with the same letter combination that does not make an *er* sound.

   Examples: first hire   pearl gear   fur pour   were here   tern steer   work pork

   a) ir _____

   b) er _____

   c) ur _____

   d) or _____

   e) ear _____

2. **Homophones** are words that sound the same, but are spelled differently. Read the word. Write its homophone on the line.

   Examples: reed   read   red   read   blew   blue

   a) rays _____   b) band _____   c) scent _____

   d) foul _____   e) board _____   f) chews _____

   g) links _____   h) hall _____   i) mussel _____

   j) heard _____   k) pause _____   l) none _____

desert	dormitory	earthworm	emergency	enormous
inspire	occurs	purchase	require	search

1. Write the correct spelling word from the list to match the clue.

a) Try to find something by looking or seeking carefully and throughly _____

b) Fill someone with the urge to do something creative _____

c) Cause to be necessary _____

d) University or college hall of residence _____

e) Burrowing worm that lives in and moves through the soil, and eats and buries decaying organic matter _____

f) Happens; takes place _____

g) Very large in size, quantity, or extent _____

h) Acquire something by paying for it; buy _____

i) Serious, unexpected, and often dangerous situation that requires immediate action _____

j) Dry area of land covered in sand, with no vegetation or water _____

The letter *r* changes the way vowels sound, such as in the words *fog* and *fort*.

The letters *or* and *ore* usually make the same sound.

Examples: torn   tore   fork   forest

The letters *ar* and *are* usually sound different.

Examples: car   care   star   stare

Say each word out loud. Listen to the sound of the vowels before the *r*. Copy and spell each word three times using colours of your choice.

1. carefully   _____   _____   _____

2. exterior   _____   _____   _____

3. unaware   _____   _____   _____

4. cookware   _____   _____   _____

5. familiar   _____   _____   _____

6. equator   _____   _____   _____

7. carnivore   _____   _____   _____

8. forest   _____   _____   _____

9. cookware   _____   _____   _____

10. necessary   _____   _____   _____

| carefully | carnivore | cookware | equator | exterior |
| familiar | forest | horizon | necessary | unaware |

1. Fill in the blank using the best spelling word from the list.

a) As we turned the corner, the houses began to look _____.

b) Hot chocolate is a _____ part of any winter gathering for my family.

c) The cat watching the bug was _____ of the dog coming behind it.

d) My family likes to watch the sun sink below the _____ at night.

e) Our scout troop went on a camping trip deep in the _____.

f) The _____ is an imaginary line around the centre of Earth.

g) Mom wrapped the gift for Grandma very _____.

h) We're buying a set of pots, pans, and other _____ for my cousin.

i) The polar bear is the largest land _____ on Earth.

j) Uncle Barry is painting the _____ of his cottage this weekend.

Brain Stretch

How many spelling words can you fit into one sentence and still make sense?
Give it a try!

Spelling Week 24 – Word Study

1. On the lines below, write these words in alphabetical order.

shark   part   ignore   torn   chore   rare   scarf   stare   forest

a) _____   b) _____   c) _____

d) _____   e) _____   f) _____

g) _____   h) _____   i) _____

2. Write a short sentence using the word below. Check your punctation.

a) spark _____

b) core _____

c) mark _____

d) fork _____

e) scare _____

f) storm _____

g) bark _____

h) tore _____

i) dare _____

1. Use the word list below to look for the words in the puzzle.

   Circle the word in the word search puzzle. Then cross out the word in the list.

F	A	R	M	E	R	A	S	B
L	S	O	R	T	E	D	M	O
A	R	P	E	C	O	O	A	R
R	I	S	N	O	R	E	R	D
E	G	C	E	U	S	S	T	E
A	N	A	R	S	E	E	R	R
H	O	R	S	E	P	D	W	E
W	R	Y	P	Y	I	A	O	H
I	E	U	A	I	K	M	R	J
B	A	R	K	I	N	G	E	K

barking	**border**	**farmer**	**flare**	**horse**	**ignore**
park	**scary**	**smart**	**snore**	**sorted**	**wore**

2. Write a word that rhymes with the word below. The word does not have to be spelled the same.

   a) tore _____

   b) shark _____

   c) corn_____

   d) share _____

   e) sports _____

   f) tarp _____

   g) sword _____

   h) parrot _____

   i) spork _____

Say each word out loud. Listen for the words that sound the same. Copy and spell each word three times using colours of your choice.

1. haul _____ _____ _____

2. creek _____ _____ _____

3. peace _____ _____ _____

4. facts _____ _____ _____

5. pain _____ _____ _____

6. creak _____ _____ _____

7. piece _____ _____ _____

8. hall _____ _____ _____

9. fax _____ _____ _____

10. pane _____ _____ _____

Brain Stretch

- Create a word search puzzle based on the spelling words.
- On a piece of paper, write a sentence using each spelling word.

creak	creek	facts	fax	hall
haul	pain	pane	peace	piece

1. Fill in the blank using the best spelling word from the list.

a) John is so hungry that he asked for a second _____ of pizza.

b) Our cat chases her toys up and down the _____ all night.

c) I tripped over a rock and cut my knee. I was in a lot of _____.

d) The board right in the middle of floor makes a really loud _____.

e) I love the _____ and quiet of an early morning breakfast.

f) My dinosaur report listed many interesting _____ about the T-rex.

g) The tow truck came to _____ away the damaged car.

h) The _____ of glass in the kitchen window is cracked.

i) We like to go down and watch minnows swim in the little _____.

j) The doctor sent the report through the _____ machine.

Brain Stretch

How many spelling words can you fit into one sentence and still make sense? Give it a try!

Spelling Week 25 – Word Study

1. **Homophones** are words that sound the same, but are spelled differently and have different meanings. Read the word. Write its homophone on the line.

a) reign _____   b) choose _____   c) scene _____

d) side _____   e) steel _____   f) piece _____

g) heard _____   h) stair _____   i) yoke _____

j) we've _____   k) vary _____   l) throne _____

2. **Homographs** are words that are spelled the same, but have different meanings and can sometimes sound different. Draw a line from the word to its meaning. You can use a dictionary, if needed.

a) lichen   to feel deep sadness about a loss

b) liken   term for morning

c) nay   period of seven days

d) neigh   slow-growing crusty plant that grows on rocks, walls, and trees

e) morn   lacking physical strength and energy

f) mourn   high-pitched sound a horse makes

g) weak   point out a resemblance to someone or something

h) week   negative answer or vote

1. Use the word list below to look for the words in the puzzle.

   Circle the word in the word search puzzle. Then cross out the word in the list.

F	L	O	W	E	R	A	F	E
C	B	W	R	I	T	E	L	X
O	I	M	A	Z	E	O	O	C
L	L	A	C	F	I	I	U	E
O	L	I	C	T	E	G	R	P
N	E	Z	W	P	H	Q	T	T
E	D	E	R	I	G	H	T	E
L	A	C	C	E	P	T	O	H
K	E	R	N	E	L	E	T	J
B	U	I	L	D	Y	U	W	Z

accept	billed	build	colonel	except	kernel
flour	flower	maize	maze	right	write

2. Draw a line to the meaning of the homophone below.

a) steal   attached or fastened with string or cord

b) steel   take something without paying for it

c) tied   rising and falling of the sea with the moon and sun

d) tide   hard, strong grey or bluish metal

Spelling Week 1 – Test

Name: _____

Listen to the spelling words. Print each spelling word.

1. _____   6. _____

2. _____   7. _____

3. _____   8. _____

4. _____   9. _____

5. _____   10. _____

Bonus

1. _____   2. _____

- -

Spelling Week 2 – Test

Name: _____

Listen to the spelling words. Print each spelling word.

1. _____   6. _____

2. _____   7. _____

3. _____   8. _____

4. _____   9. _____

5. _____   10. _____

Bonus

1. _____   2. _____

Spelling Week 3 – Test

Name: _____

Listen to the spelling words. Print each spelling word.

1. _____   6. _____

2. _____   7. _____

3. _____   8. _____

4. _____   9. _____

5. _____   10. _____

Bonus

1. _____   2. _____

- -

Spelling Week 4 – Test

Name: _____

Listen to the spelling words. Print each spelling word.

1. _____   6. _____

2. _____   7. _____

3. _____   8. _____

4. _____   9. _____

5. _____   10. _____

Bonus

1. _____   2. _____

Spelling Week 5 – Test

Name: _____

Listen to the spelling words. Print each spelling word.

1. _____   6. _____

2. _____   7. _____

3. _____   8. _____

4. _____   9. _____

5. _____   10. _____

Bonus

1. _____   2. _____

- -

Spelling Week 6 – Test

Name: _____

Listen to the spelling words. Print each spelling word.

1. _____   6. _____

2. _____   7. _____

3. _____   8. _____

4. _____   9. _____

5. _____   10. _____

Bonus

1. _____   2. _____

Spelling Week 7 – Test

Name: _____

Listen to the spelling words. Print each spelling word.

1. _____

2. _____

3. _____

4. _____

5. _____

6. _____

7. _____

8. _____

9. _____

10. _____

Bonus

1. _____

2. _____

- -

Spelling Week 8 – Test

Name: _____

Listen to the spelling words. Print each spelling word.

1. _____

2. _____

3. _____

4. _____

5. _____

6. _____

7. _____

8. _____

9. _____

10. _____

Bonus

1. _____

2. _____

Spelling Week 9 – Test

Name: _____

Listen to the spelling words. Print each spelling word.

1. _____   6. _____

2. _____   7. _____

3. _____   8. _____

4. _____   9. _____

5. _____   10. _____

Bonus

1. _____   2. _____

- -

Spelling Week 10 – Test

Name: _____

Listen to the spelling words. Print each spelling word.

1. _____   6. _____

2. _____   7. _____

3. _____   8. _____

4. _____   9. _____

5. _____   10. _____

Bonus

1. _____   2. _____

Spelling Week 11 – Test

Name: _____

Listen to the spelling words. Print each spelling word.

1. _____   6. _____

2. _____   7. _____

3. _____   8. _____

4. _____   9. _____

5. _____   10. _____

Bonus

1. _____   2. _____

- -

Spelling Week 12 – Test

Name: _____

Listen to the spelling words. Print each spelling word.

1. _____   6. _____

2. _____   7. _____

3. _____   8. _____

4. _____   9. _____

5. _____   10. _____

Bonus

1. _____   2. _____

Spelling Week 13 – Test

Name: _____

Listen to the spelling words. Print each spelling word.

1. _____   6. _____

2. _____   7. _____

3. _____   8. _____

4. _____   9. _____

5. _____   10. _____

Bonus

1. _____   2. _____

Spelling Week 14 – Test

Name: _____

Listen to the spelling words. Print each spelling word.

1. _____   6. _____

2. _____   7. _____

3. _____   8. _____

4. _____   9. _____

5. _____   10. _____

Bonus

1. _____   2. _____

Spelling Week 15 – Test

Name: _____

Listen to the spelling words. Print each spelling word.

1. _____   6. _____

2. _____   7. _____

3. _____   8. _____

4. _____   9. _____

5. _____   10. _____

Bonus

1. _____   2. _____

- -

Spelling Week 16 – Test

Name: _____

Listen to the spelling words. Print each spelling word.

1. _____   6. _____

2. _____   7. _____

3. _____   8. _____

4. _____   9. _____

5. _____   10. _____

Bonus

1. _____   2. _____

Spelling Week 17 – Test

Name: _____

Listen to the spelling words. Print each spelling word.

1. _____   6. _____

2. _____   7. _____

3. _____   8. _____

4. _____   9. _____

5. _____   10. _____

Bonus

1. _____   2. _____

- -

Spelling Week 18 – Test

Name: _____

Listen to the spelling words. Print each spelling word.

1. _____   6. _____

2. _____   7. _____

3. _____   8. _____

4. _____   9. _____

5. _____   10. _____

Bonus

1. _____   2. _____

Spelling Week 19 – Test

Name: _____

Listen to the spelling words. Print each spelling word.

1. _____   6. _____

2. _____   7. _____

3. _____   8. _____

4. _____   9. _____

5. _____   10. _____

Bonus

1. _____   2. _____

- -

Spelling Week 20 – Test

Name: _____

Listen to the spelling words. Print each spelling word.

1. _____   6. _____

2. _____   7. _____

3. _____   8. _____

4. _____   9. _____

5. _____   10. _____

Bonus

1. _____   2. _____

Spelling Week 21 – Test

Name: _____

Listen to the spelling words. Print each spelling word.

1. _____   6. _____

2. _____   7. _____

3. _____   8. _____

4. _____   9. _____

5. _____   10. _____

Bonus

1. _____   2. _____

Spelling Week 22 – Test

Name: _____

Listen to the spelling words. Print each spelling word.

1. _____   7. _____

2. _____   8. _____

3. _____   9. _____

4. _____   10. _____

5. _____   11. _____

6. _____   12. _____

Spelling Week 23 – Test   Name: _____

Listen to the spelling words. Print each spelling word.

1. _____   6. _____

2. _____   7. _____

3. _____   8. _____

4. _____   9. _____

5. _____   10. _____

Bonus

1. _____   2. _____

- -

Spelling Week 24 – Test   Name: _____

Listen to the spelling words. Print each spelling word.

1. _____   6. _____

2. _____   7. _____

3. _____   8. _____

4. _____   9. _____

5. _____   10. _____

Bonus

1. _____   2. _____

Spelling Week 25 – Test

Name: _____

Listen to the spelling words. Print each spelling word.

1. _____   6. _____

2. _____   7. _____

3. _____   8. _____

4. _____   9. _____

5. _____   10. _____

Bonus

1. _____   2. _____

- -

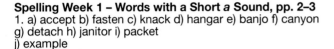

Spelling Week 1 – Words with a Short *a* Sound, pp. 2–3
1. a) accept b) fasten c) knack d) hangar e) banjo f) canyon
g) detach h) janitor i) packet
j) example

Spelling Week 1 – Word Study, p. 4
1. a) packet b) fasten c) hangar d) detach e) banjo f) janitor
g) canyon h) example
2. a) knack b) fasten c) detach d) hangar e) example f)
janitor g) canyon h) accept
3. a) ankle b) happy c) smacked d) always e) having

Spelling Week 1 – Word Study, p. 5
1. a) janitor b) banjo c) knack d) hangar e) detach f) example
g) packet h) fasten i) canyon
j) accept
2. a) track, past, half b) cackle, blank, habitat c) laugh,
splash, crabby

Spelling Week 2 – Words with a Short *e* Sound, pp. 6–7
1. a) exercise b) medicine c) shorten d) sketch e) impatient f)
venom g) petition h) quartet
i) regular j) television

Spelling Week 2 – Word Study, p. 8
1. a) special, propel, letter b) spending, fresher, feather,
melt c) fender, lemon, health d) barrette, shred, elephant e)
friend, crept, vest
2. a) felt b) sketch c) cabinet d) crept
3. Sample answers: A lumberjack can fell a tree very
quickly. I fell while I was trying to climb a brick wall.

Spelling Week 2 – Word Study, p. 9
1. a) petition b) venom c) television d) sketch e) shorten f)
regular g) exercise h) quartet
i) medicine j) impatient
2. Sample answers: a) fell, smell, shell, swell, tell, yell b)
wealth c) kept

Spelling Week 3 – Words with a Short *i* Sound, pp. 10–11
1. a) predict b) accident c) cabinet d) fossil e) official f)
resident g) skillet h) listening i) exhibit
j) ignore

Spelling Week 3 – Word Study, p. 12
1. a) imagine b) comic c) bridge
2. a) practice b) mist c) which d) guilt e) lynx f) ring
3. a) 2 syllables b) 5 syllables c) 2 syllables
4. Sample answers: a) willed, filled, billed, gild, guild, build,
killed, grilled, skilled b) bit, mitt, spit, kit, knit, nit, fit, sit c)
sift, lift, rift, miffed d) kitten, bitten e) glitter, bitter, sitter,
fitter, spitter, flitter
f) flip, lip, drip, ship, hip, nip, rip, whip, trip, sip, tip, clip

Spelling Week 3 – Word Study, p. 13
1.

2. a) skillet b) ignore c) predict d) official e) exhibit f) cabinet

**Spelling Week 4 – Words with a Short *o* Sound, pp.
14–15**
1. a) adopt b) project c) copier d) blonde e) solve f) voluntary
g) bonnet h) knowledge i) involve
j) following

Spelling Week 4 – Word Study, p. 16
1. a) solve b) adopt c) project d) bonnet
2. Sample answers: a) stopped, popped, flopped, cropped,
dropped b) lock, clock, knock, shock, crock, talk, walk,
rock, stock c) drop, flop, shop, crop d) lot, hot, got, rot,
shot, brought, fought, ought, caught e) loss, boss, sauce,
floss, gloss, cross f) lawn, shone, on g) revolve, evolve,
dissolve h) wallow, swallow, hollow i) sloppy, floppy, poppy,
choppy, gloppy
3. a) bossy, tonic, softly b) tropical, cross, fought c) rocket,
brought, fossil

Spelling Week 4 – Word Study, p. 17
1. a) blonde b) involve c) project d) adopt e) bonnet f) copier
g) voluntary h) following i) coffee
j) solve
2. a) a) project b) adopt c blonde d) involve e) coffee f)
copier

**Spelling Week 5 – Words with a Short *u* Sound, pp.
18–19**
1. a) punish b) culture c) support d) luggage e) sculptor f)
button g) plumber h) muscle i) tuxedo
j) crutch

Spelling Week 5 – Word Study, p. 20
1. a) proud, through b) pounce, cough c) about, fruit d)
though, guest
2. Sample answers: a) thunder, plunder, blunder b) glove,
shove, love, above, dove d) puff, fluff, muff, cuff, scuff
d) puddle, muddle e) stumble, tumble, crumble, bumble,
rumble f) rough, tough, enough
3. a) tuxedo b) sculptor c) culture d) muscle e) crutch f)
button g) plumber h) luggage i) punish

Spelling Week 5 – Word Study, p. 21
1.

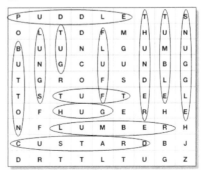

2. Sample answers: a) ton, shun, fun, one, done, won,
run, spun, stun b) rough, cuff, scuff, muff, fluff c) gummy,
mummy, dummy, crummy d) humble, bumble, tumble,
stumble, crumble
e) thunder, wonder, under, plunder f) lumpy, stumpy, dumpy,
bumpy

Spelling Week 6 – Words with a Long *a* Sound, pp. 22–23
1. a) capable b) detail c) gaze d) halo e) imitate f) elevator g)
grateful h) waste i) mistake
j) Ancient (it's okay if they don't use a capital)

Spelling Week 6 – Word Study, p. 24
1. a) crate, make, stale b) stake, hazy, slate c) taste, rain,
frame d) parade, lake, away
2. Sample answers: table, chair, slate, bookcase, crayons,
paper, crate, paints, paintbrushes, trays, plates, shoelaces,
cables, faces, cases, pencil cases
3. Stories will vary. You may wish to ask some children to
share with the class or with a partner.

Spelling Week 6 – Word Study, p. 25
1.

(word search grid)

2. Sample answers: a) care, bear, rare, air, stare, stair, share,
dare, pear, pare, hair b) take, sake, fake, make, ache, lake,
rake, shake c) came, tame, lame, fame, shame, frame,
flame, game
d) taste, waist, paste, paced, raced, aced, erased, waste e)
day, say, ray, lay, way, hay, stay, may, pay, delay, fray, pray,
prey f) gain, main, lane, rain, sane, cane, again, plane, plain,
strain, crane, pain, brain, drain

Spelling Week 7 – Words with a Long *e* Sound, pp. 26–27
1. a) release b) weevil c) zero d) yield e) defeat f) ceiling g)
fierce h) museum i) creative j) beliefs
Spelling Week 7 – Word Study, p. 28
1. a) museumb) weevil c) defeat d) fierce e) beliefs f) yield g)
ceiling h) creative i) release
2. a) field, mean, alley b) relief, event, greet c) tweezers,
bunny, cleaver d) create, rely e) speech, seek, fairy
3. a) cart/wheel, beach/ball, earth/quake b) day/dream, sea/
star, fire/works c) ear/lobe, honey/dew, sting/ray d) tea/
spoon, time/line, pony/tail

Spelling Week 7 – Word Study, p. 29
1. a) ceiling b) beliefs c) creative d) weevil e) yield f) zero g)
defeat h) release i) fierce j) museum
2. Sample answers: a) feed, speech, seek, leek, keen, seen,
been, free, greet, greedy b) field, believe, belief, brief, chief,
niece, priest, siege, achieve, piece c) funny, bunny, runny,
sunny, monkey, donkey, galley, alley, valley, money d) weak,
dear, fear, gear, leaf, steal, meal, real, deal, heal, seal, zeal,
appeal, squeal, read, teach, reach

Spelling Week 8 – Words with a Long *i* Sound, pp. 30–31
1. a) frighten b) outline c) choir d) fireproof e) knives f)
pastime g) crisis h) entire i) invite j) remind

Spelling Week 8 – Word Study, p. 32
1. a) spine, sigh, lightning b) bright, style, fry c) signed,
rhyme, write d) chime, cycle, twine
e) twice, fried, height
2. a) string b) timid
3. a) cacti b) outline c) shines d) invited e) climb

Spelling Week 8 – Word Study, p. 33
1
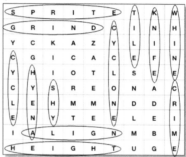

2. Sample answers: a) line, spine, mine, wine, whine, fine b)
like, trike, bike, pike, hike c) lie, die, cry, sigh, dry, fry, spy,
shy, try, lye d) while, file, mile, bile, smile, pile, trial e) height,
white, right, write, bright, might, sprite, fright, kite, bite, site,
sight f) wide, slide, cried, fried, dried, pride

Spelling Week 9 – Words with a Long *o* Sound, pp. 34–35
1. a) loaves b) remote c) ratio d) solar e) piano f) quote g)
owner h) roam i) envelope j) poem

Spelling Week 9 – Word Study, p. 36
1. A Giant Oak stood near a brook in which grew some
slender Reeds. When the wind blew, the great Oak stood
proudly upright with its hundred arms uplifted to the sky.
But the Reeds bowed low in the wind and sang a sad and
mournful song.
"You have reason to complain," said the Oak. "The slightest
breeze that ruffles the surface of the water makes you bow
your heads, while I, the mighty Oak, stand upright and firm
before the howling tempest."
   "Do not worry about us," replied the Reeds. "The winds do
not harm us. We bow before them and so we do not break.
You, in all your pride and strength, have so far resisted their
blows. But the end is coming."
   As the Reeds spoke, a great hurricane rushed out of the
north. The Oak stood proudly and fought against the storm,
while the yielding Reeds bowed low. The wind redoubled in
fury, and all at once the great tree fell, torn up by the roots, and
lay among the pitying Reeds.
Moral: Better to yield [stop resisting] when it is folly
[foolishness] to resist, than to resist stubbornly and be
destroyed.
2. a) far b) thawed
3. hung loosely and gracefully

Spelling Week 9 – Word Study, p. 37
1. a) roam b) poem c) envelope d) owner e) piano f) solar g)
remote h) quote i) ratio j) loaves
2. Sample answers: a) toe, foe, hoe, doe, oboe, woe b)
float, boat, coat, goat, moat, stoat, oat, groan, toast, goal,

loaf, load, road, roam c) grow, glow, flow, know, show, slow, snow, growth, narrow, sparrow, furrow, barrow, tomorrow d) go, no, so, banjo, bonus, focus, comb, total, piano, solo, trio (Note: Words with a consonant + e are also acceptable. Sample answers: bone, tone, phone, alone, stroke, stole, store, etc.)

Spelling Week 10 – Words with a Long *u* Sound, pp. 38–39
1. a) review b) interview c) barbecue d) ambulance e) immune f) mute g) rescue h) fuel i) musician j) vacuum

Spelling Week 10 – Word Study, p. 40
1. a) rescue, cue, unite b) university, menu, yule c) chew, music, argue d) rescue, view, unique
2. Sample answers: The human eye has a black pupil. My teacher says I am a very good pupil.
3. Sample answers: I try hard to communicate with my baby sister, but she doesn't talk yet. My best friend and I communicate very well in our secret language.

Spelling Week 10 – Word Study, p. 41
1.

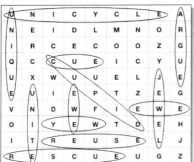

Spelling Week 11 – Words with *y* as Long *i* and Long *e* Sounds, pp. 42–43
1. a) poultry b) hyphen c) reply d) notify e) injury f) electricity g) buyer h) directory i) alchemy j) deny

Spelling Week 11 – Word Study, p. 44
1. a) circle: guy, cry; underline: many, plenty b) circle: rely, recycle; underline: smelly, eventually c) circle: bylaw, apply; underline: twenty, carry d) circle: deny, spy; underline: alley, history
e) circle: style, rely; underline: hungry, angry f) circle: kayak, verify; underline: fairy, cherry
2. a) hair + cut, night + mare b) no + body, cave + man c) dragon + fly, fire + cracker

Spelling Week 11 – Word Study, p. 45
1. a) notify b) directory c) deny d) alchemy e) injury f) reply g) buyer h) poultry i) electricity j) hyphen
2. Sample answers: I type my school work on my laptop. An oxeye daisy is a type of wildflower.

Spelling Week 12 – Contractions, pp. 46–47
1. a) she'd b) they'll c) I've d) couldn't e) we've f) won't g) you're h) couldn't i) haven't j) he'll

Spelling Week 12 – Word Study, p. 48

1. a) circle "willn't"; won't b) circle "cann't"; can't c) circle "willn't"; won't d) circle "cant"; can't
e) circle "Donot"; Don't f) circle "Hasnot"; Hasn't
2. a) could not b) has not c) we are d) she had or she would e) that is f) do not g) cannot h) will not
i) you will j) he is or he has

Spelling Week 12 – Word Study, p. 49
1.

Full Word	Contractions
are	you're, they're, we're
am	I'm
will	I'll, you'll, they'll, she'll, he'll, we'll
has or is	he's, she's
would or had	he'd, she'd, they'd, we'd, I'd, you'd
have	you've, they've, we've, I've

2. a) couldn't b) wasn't c) hasn't d) won't e) can't f) shouldn't

Spelling Week 13 – Double Consonants, pp. 50–51
1. a) forgetting b) crystallize c) appreciate d) happiness e) discuss f) immediately g) dessert h) marriage i) common j) manner

Spelling Week 13 – Word Study, p. 52
1. a) fussed, fussing b) knitted, knitting c) shrugged, shrugging d) planted, planting e) travelled, travelling
2. a) **X**; glowing b) ✔ c) ✔ d) **X**; mashing e) **X**; marvelled f) **X**; sweating g) ✔ h) **X**; talking

Spelling Week 13 – Word Study, p. 53
1.

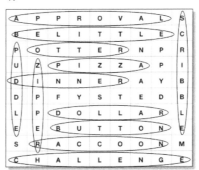

2. Sample answers: a) ball, wall, tall, crawl, mall, drawl, call, shawl, fall, haul, squall, stall
b) bitter, fitter, sitter, litter, twitter, spitter c) spill, fill, twill, grill, pill, sill, frill, bill, will d) fatter, patter, spatter, splatter, shatter, batter, clatter e) loss, moss, toss, cross, floss f) flutter, butter, mutter, shutter, sputter g) runny, funny, bunny, money, honey h) bell, spell, fell, swell, well, sell, gel, tell, smell i) fist, mist, kissed, twist, wrist, hissed, list, grist, resist, untwist, insist, enlist, dismissed

Spelling Week 14 – Words with Silent Letters, pp. 54–55
1. a) league b) daylight c) wrinkle d) rehearse e) autumn f) cologne g) athlete h) descent i) salmon j) knead

Answers

Spelling Week 14 – Word Study, p. 56
1. a) an<u>ch</u>or, <u>h</u>onest, ras<u>p</u>berry b) ballet, design, fasten
c) <u>ch</u>emical, <u>g</u>uard, debri<u>s</u> d) an<u>s</u>wer, <u>s</u>cience, bris<u>t</u>les e)
peo<u>p</u>le, <u>g</u>nome, plumber, ton<u>gue</u>
2. a) shame b) grade c) scare d) cute e) robe f) scrape g)
grime h) plane
3. Sample answer: When I add an *e*, the vowel changes
from a short sound to a long sound.
4. a) L b) S c) L d) L e) S f) L g) S h) L

Spelling Week 14 – Word Study, p. 57
1. a) knead b) salmon c) league d) daylight e) rehearse f)
autumn g) wrinkle h) athlete i) descent
j) cologne
2. Sample answers: a) write, wrong, wriggle, wrap, wrist,
wrinkle, wreck, wreath, wren, wrestle
b) ghost, though, although, eight, weight, height, high,
thigh, knight, neighbour, neigh c) comb, bomb, tomb, climb,
limb, lamb, thumb, plumber d) glisten, listen, hustle, wrestle,
bristle, bustle, nestle, rustle, thistle, whistle, trestle

Spelling Week 15 – Words with Long and Short *oo*
Sounds, pp. 58–59
1. a) smoothie b) outlook c) notebook d) bookshelf e)
kangaroo f) raccoon g) foolish h) shampoo i) wooden j)
footstool

Spelling Week 15 – Word Study, p. 60
1. a) tuna, crew, glue b) route, dune, fruit c) plume, noodle,
renew d spruce, soup, scuba
2. a) pudding, should, woman b) wool, puss, fulcrum c)
cookie, sugar, bull d) push, butcher, octopus
3. a) S b) N c) L d) N e) L f) S g) N h) S i) L

Spelling Week 15 – Word Study, p. 61
1.

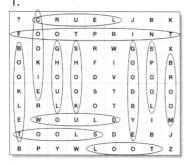

2. Sample answers: a) boot, route, suit, scoot, root, loot,
shute, fruit b) crook, took, look, hook, nook, shook, cook,
book c) moon, soon, rune, prune, balloon, dune, goon,
baboon, soon
d) room, bloom, plume, tomb, womb, loom, boom e) full,
wool, bull, awful f) grew, blue, blew, knew, new, crew, due,
sue, flu, flew, flue, true, shoo, shoe, glue, flue, flu g) pool,
tool, cool, stool, fool, rule, school h) could, good, would,
stood, understood, wood i) moose, goose, loose

Spelling Week 16 – Words with *oi* and *oy*, pp. 62–63
1. a) noisy b) asteroid c) choice d) destroy e) voyage f) loyal
g) moisture h) avoid i) oyster j) enjoy

Spelling Week 16 – Word Study, p. 64
1. a) cowboy b) noisy c) gargoyle d) choice e) destroy f)
oysters g) spoiled
2. Sample answers: a) baseball, basketball, softball,
football, snowball b) brainwash, brainwave, brainstorm,
brainfog c) bookworm, bookshelf, bookcase, bookmark,
bookstore d) mailbox, inbox, lunchbox, breadbox, outbox,
toolbox, dropbox, cashbox, kickbox, sandbox, jukebox,
skybox, hatbox, shoebox, matchbox, lockbox e) friendship,
leadership, membership, hardship, kinship, relationship,
citizenship, internship, partnership, scholarship, fellowship,
viewership, readership, listenership f) something, someone,
somebody, sometime, someplace, somewhere, someday,
somehow, somewhat g) dragonfly, butterfly, shadfly,
mayfly, blackfly, deerfly, housefly, whitefly h) bedroom,
bedsheets, bedpan, bedspread, bedclothes, bedposts,
bedtime, bedrock, bedside i) sunlight, sunshine, sunflower,
sunbeam, sundog, sunlit, Sunday, sunburn, sunglasses,
sunfish, sunroof, sunrise, sunset j) myself, itself, herself,
himself, yourself k) firefighter, fireman, fireplace, fireworks,
firebrand, firebreak, firelight, fireproof, firecracker l) eyeball,
eyebrow, eyelashes, eyesight, eyeshadow, eyeliner, eyelid,
eyeglasses

Spelling Week 16 – Word Study, p. 65
1. a) spoiled b) oysters c) asteroid d) noisy e) cowboy f)
voyage g) choice h) destroy i) gargoyle
j) coiled
2. Sample answers: a) joint, point, coin, android, toilet, boil,
soil, toil, voice, oink, noise b) joy, royal, toy, soy, coy, boy,
ahoy, annoy, alloy, employ

Spelling Week 17 – Words with *ow* and *ou*, pp. 66–67
1. a) trowel b) shower c) downspout d) thousand e) drowsy
f) announce g) flounder h) chowder
i) discount j) surrounded

Spelling Week 17 – Word Study, p. 68
1. a) underline: plough, crowd, allow; circle: although, glow
b) underline: shout, aloud; circle: pillow, narrow, borrow c)
underline: slouch, scowl, trout; circle: sparrow, snowball d)
underline: bounce, fountain, tower; circle: throw, shallow
2. a) pleasant taste similar to sugar or honey b) set of rooms
for an individual's or family's use, or for a particular purpose
c) yellow internal part of an animal's or bird's egg d) wooden
crosspiece fastened over the necks of two animals and
attached to a cart or plough for pulling e) mixture of gases
living things need to live f) person entitled to inherit specific
property g) part of the human body betwee the ribs and
hips h) use carelessly or for no reason; discarded materials

Spelling Week 17 – Word Study, p. 69
1.

2. Sample answers: a) shallow, mallow, tallow, wallow b) clown, down, town, drown, frown, brown, gown, sown c) sour, tour d) fowl, cowl, owl, scowl, bowl e) found, sound, round, ground, bound, wound f) flower, power, tower, glower, blower g) mouth h) proud, loud, shroud i) mouse, house

Spelling Week 18 – Words with an *s* Sound: c and *s*, pp. 70–71
1. a) juicy b) possible c) promise d) instead e) saucer f) crystal g) exciting h) earliest i) entrance
j) scissors

Spelling Week 18 – Word Study, p. 72
1. a) phrase, organism, measure b) cousin, dessert, wisdom c) business, clothes, vision
d) cheese, raise, poison
2. a) nearby b) shut something c) material thing that can be seen and touched d) say something to express disapproval or disagreement with something e) to lessen the blame for something
f) poor reason for having done something g) injury in which the skin is cut or broken h) repeatedly twisted or coiled something around itself or a core; turned a key repeatedly to make a clock, watch, or clockwork object operate

Spelling Week 18 – Word Study, p. 73
1.

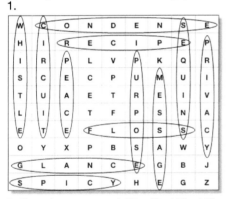

2. Sample answers: a) lift, gift, drift, shift, miffed b) mice, nice, spice, rice, dice, twice c) glance, lance, prance, ants, aunts d) list, missed, fist, mist, twist e) mace, lace, face, race, pace, case, space, trace, grace, bass, base f) mess, bless, caress, dress, confess, press, stress g) west, pest, messed, best, rest, nest, test h) loose, moose, goose, caboose, spruce i) cider, rider, strider, wider, divider, guider, collider, glider

Spelling Week 19 – Words with a *j* Sound: g and *j*, pp. 74–75
1. a) Junior (it's okay if they don't use a capital) b) jacket c) allergy d) strategy e) judge
f) imaginary g) contagious h) manager i) sponge j) gigantic

Spelling Week 19 – Word Study, p. 76
1. a) angle, girl b) organic, ringer c) gardener, guard d) geese, wriggle
2. You may wish to invite a few children to share their paragraphs with the class.

Spelling Week 19 – Word Study, p. 77
1. a) sponge b) junior c) allergy d) imaginary e) manager f) gigantic g) contagious h) judge
i) strategy j) jacket
2. Sample answers: a) jingle, jungle, jump, jive, jiggle, jog, job b) fudge, nudge, budge, edge, ledge, age, rage, sage, dodge, danger, range, ranger, stranger c) ginseng, ginger, giant, digit, religion, religious, region, legion d) smudgy, fudgy, edgy, spongy, strategy, technology, apology

Spelling Week 20 – Words with an *f* Sound Spelled *ph, gh,* and *f*, pp. 78–79
1. a) relief b) telephone c) Safety d) enough e) trophies f) elephant g) cough h) physical i) prefer
j) tough

Spelling Week 20 – Word Study, p. 80
1. Sample answers: a) ice cubes; icicles b) firey orange ball; fireball c) perfume; heaven
d) warm hug; cozy blanket e) butterflies; fairies; dancers f) a wild horse; a raging lion g) crashing cymbals; drum rolls
2. a) plenty b) calmness
3. a) danger b) genuine

Spelling Week 20 – Word Study, p. 81
1.

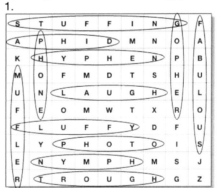

2. Sample answers: a) half, staff, laugh, calf b) rough, tough, fluff, cuff, scuff, enough
c) lake, fake, shake, brake, break, take, cake, sake, bake, wake, sake, ache, mistake, quake, earthquake d) meal, feel, wheel, congeal, reel, real, teal, squeal, peal e) judge, nudge, grudge, smudge, sludge, budge f) alone, shown, crone, blown, thrown, drone g) linx, stinks, inks, sinks, rinks, minks, shrinks, slinks h) pinch, winch, cinch, flinch i) smile, while, isle, aisle, style, pile, dial, trial, bile

Spelling Week 21 – Consonant Digraphs: *ch, sh, th,* and *wh*, pp. 82–83
1. a) strength b) character c) mythology d) establish e) shelves f) exchange g) shampoo
i) whether j) Whose

Spelling Week 21 – Word Study, p. 84
1. a) bunch b) thought c) shingles d) sixth e) dish f) church g) throat h) whole i) thing j) whisper
k) squash l) check
2. Sample answers: a) whip, ship, chip b) chick, thick c)

wish, with d) chat, that, what e) then, when f) chin, shin, thin
g) cheat, wheat h) chose, those, whose

Spelling Week 21 – Word Study, p. 85
1. a) strength b) exchange c) shelves d) whether e) establish
f) mythology g) theme h) shampoo
i) whose j) character

Spelling Week 22 – Consonant Blends: *scr, spl, spr,* and *str,* pp. 86–87
1. a) strive b) struggle c) screech d) display e) splice f)
sprained g) instruction h) screen
i) sprinkle j) splatter

Spelling Week 22 – Word Study, p. 88
1. a) tuna, blew, true b) glue, crew, fruit c) pool, loose, due
d) review, soup, loom
2. a) stood, could, look b) soot, should, woof c) hood,
wood, pull d) cookie, brook, foot
3. a) S b) N c) L d) L e) N f) S g) N h) S i) L

Spelling Week 22 – Word Study, p. 89
1.

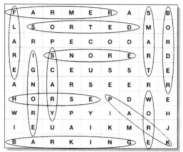

2. a) scrunch b) street c) spritz d) stream e) scrub f) splat g)
script h) sprayer i) strength j) sprout k) stripes l) spread

**Spelling Week 23 – *R*-controlled Vowels with *or, er, ir, ur,*
and *ear,* pp. 90–91**
1. a) purchase b) dormitory c) enormous d) search e) inspire
f) desert g) earthworm h) emergency i) occurs j) require

Spelling Week 23 – Word Study, p. 92
1. Sample answers: a) whirr, fir, stir, sir, twirl, girl; sire, fire,
wire, tire, expire b) term, germ, fern
c) blur, purr, sure, burst, burn, burp, during, curl; bury, fury,
four, pour, course, court, source, lure
d) worm, world, word, worse, worst, work; born, torn, tore,
sore, shore, more, sorry, for, fort, fork, forty e) learn, heard,
pearl, early, earth, earthquake; bear, clear, tear, pear, hear,
shear, fear
f) were; where, nowhere, here, mere, sphere, adhere, severe
2. a) raise b) banned c) cent or sent d) fowl e) bored f)
choose g) lynx h) haul i) muscle j) herd
k) paws l) nun

Spelling Week 23 – Word Study, p. 93
1. a) search b) inspire c) require d) dormitory e) earthworm f)
occurs g) enormous h) purchase
i) emergency j) desert

**Spelling Week 24 – *R*-controlled Vowels with *ar, are, or,*
and *ore,* pp. 94–95**

1. a) familiar b) necessary c) unaware d) horizon e) forest f)
equator g) carefully h) cookware
i) carnivore j) exterior

Spelling Week 24 – Word Study, p. 96
1. a) chore b) forest c) ignore d) part e) rare f) scarf g) shark
h) stare i) torn
2. You may wish to invite children to share some of their
sentences with the class.

Spelling Week 24 – Word Study, p. 97
1.

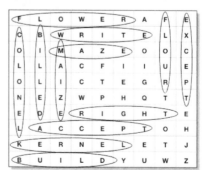

2. Sample answers: a) score, swore, wore, store, shore,
more, sore, bore, wore b) lark, mark, ark, bark, park, spark
c) worn, born, torn, morn, horn d) mare, care, hair, hare, fair,
fare, scare, stare, spare, pear, bear, lair, stair, glare, aware e)
shorts, courts, ports, sorts, forts, skorts, warts f) carp, harp
g) ford, bored, award, lord, scored, roared, gored, chord,
cored h) ferret, merit, caret i) fork, pork, torque

**Spelling Week 25 – Homographs and Homophones, pp.
98–99**
1. a) piece b) hall c) pain d) creak e) peace f) facts g) haul h)
pane i) creek j) fax

Spelling Week 25 – Word Study, p. 100
1. a) rain or rein b) chews c) seen d) sighed e) steal f) peace
g) herd h) stare i) yolk j) weave
k) very l) thrown
2. a) slow-growing crusty plant that grows on rocks, walls,
and trees b) point out a resemblance to someone or
something c) negative answer or vote d) high-pitched sound
a horse makes
e) term for morning f) to feel deep sadness about a loss
g) lacking physical strength and energy h) period of seven
days

Spelling Week 25 – Word Study, p. 101
1.

2. a) take something without paying for it b) hard, strong
grey or bluish metal c) attached or fastened with string or
cord d) rising and falling of the sea with the moon and sun